CLASSROOM DISCIPLINE AND CONTROL:

101 practical techniques

also by the authors

CLASSROOM DISCIPLINE AND CONTROL:

101 practical techniques

Fred B. Chernow
Carol Chernow

Parker Publishing Company, Inc.

West Nyack, New York

© 1981, by

PARKER PUBLISHING COMPANY, INC.
West Nyack, New York

19   18

Library of Congress Cataloging in Publication Data

Chernow, Fred B.
    Classroom discipline and control.

    Includes index.
    1. Classroom management—Handbooks, manuals, etc.
I. Chernow, Carol,   joint author.   II. Title.
LB3013.C47   371.1'024   80-21700
ISBN 0-13-136283-6

Printed in the United States of America

acknowledgments

Above all to our students: ranging from first graders at Fort Meade, Maryland to undergraduates at St. John's University, Staten Island. They are clearly the *sine qua non* of this book. In teaching them we learned much.

Two educators: Community Superintendent *Louis De Sario* and Supervising Principal *Bernard Walker*, both of whom put into practice each day the best in modern educational theory and research. They continue to inspire us.

We wish to express our gratitude to our daughters *Barbara* and *Lynne*, now grown, who, throughout their childhood years, taught us that the best discipline comes from within.

Finally, a special debt, incalculable as it is unpayable, to our own parents and teachers who taught us how important and permanent are the habits and attitudes acquired during the early years.

F.B.C.
C.C.

how this book will help the classroom teacher

Do you occasionally feel that you are a referee instead of a teacher? One teacher we know said she sometimes felt the need for a whip and chair rather than for a lesson plan. There may not be a direct problem between you and the students—sometimes the problem is that the students simply cannot get along with one another.

Classroom management is one of the most perplexing problems facing experienced teachers all over the country. Perennially, the Gallup Poll indicates that discipline is viewed nationally as the Number One concern. This handbook offers a comprehensive collection of ready-to-use, successful strategies that prevent discipline problems *before* they start and it will also help you take control when trouble erupts in spite of your best efforts. You will find here a complete, helpful assortment of indispensible classroom techniques, suggestions and ideas, including many practical tips that will be news even to veteran teachers.

All the techniques and approaches will be applicable to any size group—any grade—any subject. These tested control factors will put you squarely in the driver's seat, enabling you to gain the respect and attention of every pupil in your class.

What psychological price are you now paying in an attempt to control your class? However high the price may be, here are eight reasons why this could be the most important book in your professional library.

Using just some of its provocative and proven ideas will help you to:

   . . . improve pupil performance

   . . . relieve fatigue

   . . . cut down on disruptions

   . . . provide *lasting* motivation

   . . . increase your satisfaction in the classroom

   . . . save instructional time

   . . . build mutual respect

   . . . provide a happier, more productive classroom environment

In Chapter 4, for example, you will learn to use body language rather than a raised voice to get a "difficult" youngster to comply. Let's say Jimmy continues to talk to a neighbor during a silent reading period—after you've told him to get busy. You can assert yourself by raising your voice *or*, as we show you, by simply making a gesture.

The important thing to get across is that you mean it when you say: "Everyone WILL read this book." If Jimmy gets away with not following your orders today, several others will try it tomorrow. If you go to write on the chalkboard or return to your desk with a half-hearted admonition, *nothing* is likely to change. This chapter shows you how to use such silent but effective methods as: the steely stare and the "lethal lean." None of these methods require you to touch the child or use your voice, but all work. Even more important, they establish your control. You quickly get a reputation for "meaning business" and not for being a "screamer" or "pushover." Best of all, you don't go home with a sore throat or bruised ego!

A distraught teacher begins a note to the principal with: "I had trip money in my desk and it was stolen. I know that I shouldn't keep money in my desk but . . ." In Chapter 2 you will learn of six ways you can prevent stealing *before* it happens.

Your pupils will enjoy school more as you assume firm but friendly control of the classroom situation. Starting with Chapter 1, you will learn how to develop a "command presence" without making empty threats. The Seven Roads to Trouble are identified for you so that you can undo some of the contradictory messages you may be transmitting to your pupils now.

The area of "conflict management" is discussed in Chapter 3. Here you will learn to handle the "choreographer"—the pupil who enjoys setting up confrontations between other pupils while remaining in the background. This chapter alone can help you eliminate a repetition of those days when you went home with a headache due to noise, stress, and verbal abuse.

Dozens of successful teachers have developed and refined these approaches with their classes—turning disruptive children into eager, cooperative learners. You will find an abundance of voice-saving, problem-solving tips and methods which you'll want to put to use immediately. Among them are:

- *Suggestions* for setting limits; making your class know they may go just so far and no further.
- *Practices* which have proven successful in classrooms just like yours.
- *Hints* on how to use your voice forcefully without getting shrill or booming.
- *Tips* on what you can do to reward those pupils who are behaving and want to work.
- *Examples* of good and poor methods of punishment and follow-up.
- *Activities* and *ideas* for keeping pupils busy in a meaningful way—and out of trouble.

In addition, you'll discover answers to these six questions that baffle so many good teachers:

1. How can I encourage pupils to behave and work *with* me?
2. How can I discipline individual offenders?
3. How can I minimize group infractions or misbehavior?
4. How can I deal with behavior problems that can't be settled in class?
5. How can I get pupils to work with me not because they *have* to but because they *want* to?
6. How can I handle specific types of disciplinary infractions such as:

constant talking	foul language
open defiance	room leaving
refusal to do work	pupil fights
horseplay	stealing

As you know, good intentions are not enough. The best lesson plans fall on deaf ears if you don't have good control. Good teachers need a wide range of skills and specific, concrete examples of how to cope in the classroom with the pupil of today. How to attain and use such skills is the main theme of this book.

Instead of staring at the clock and wondering when the bell will ring, apply these strategies that have proven to work in classrooms just like yours. Here is a valuable handbook brimming over with tactics and devices sure to lighten your load. It will save you countless hours of threats, scowls, and shouts as you deal with the many unpredictable problems that all teachers face daily.

The dozens of sanity-saving approaches will lighten your burden and increase your effectiveness. As another example, Chapter 9 contains action-getting form letters to parents that you can fill out and prepare for mailing in a matter of minutes. Some are sequential, with the tone of each follow-up a little more severe. Others ask for the parent's signature and are worded to get total and prompt cooperation.

Classroom management by a calm teacher will make a great difference to your pupils, especially to those who have not felt confident in school before. The many case histories of aggressive children and how they have been successfully handled will encourage you to put these 101 ideas to work—immediately.

Fred B. Chernow
Carol Chernow

contents

15 solving attendance problems related to discipline 187

Index 199

1

establishing control
the very first day

Are you a new teacher with stars in your eyes and butterflies in your stomach? Perhaps you are an experienced teacher in a new school system, or even a veteran teacher about to enter the classroom for the twelfth time. In any case, new pupils and new challenges await you. These days the emphasis is on the word *challenge*. More and more pupils tend to challenge the authority of their teachers. Are you ready for them? This chapter will help you with proven ideas and tested suggestions to meet these challenges.

how to prepare for "day one"

Anticipate everything that can come up on the first day of the term. In case of a fire drill, will you know how to lead your class out of the building? What is the bell schedule? Will you know when to expect the lunch bell and when it is dismissal time? In case a pupil needs the nurse, do you know where her office is?

Get to know the school plant. Locate the exits and staircases that your pupils will be expected to use. If you will need additional textbooks and supplies, where can you send for them? In case a child gets sick in the room, where can you get a custodial worker to clean up? If it rains on the first day of school, where will you pick your class up?

Get off on the right foot by preparing your room to welcome its new pupil-occupants. A cluttered or barren room sends a negative message to your pupils. A well-organized, attractive room gives an "in-control" image that pupils respect. It will be well worth the extra effort to set your room up in advance of "day one." On one area of the bulletin board, list some class rules, such as, *Stand when you speak; Place coats in the closet; No sharpening pencils after the late bell; No gum chewing;* etc. On another bulletin board, list some topics or units of work that will be studied. Pupils like to have a preview of what lies ahead. If you have very young pupils, place name labels over their coat hooks. If you have intermediate grade pupils, put name labels on the pupils' desks. This tells the children right away that you expect them to take the same hook or seat every day. A simple "constant" like this gives security even to pupils who may have a great deal of chaos in their home lives.

If your room has movable furniture, be sure to align all the desks on the first day. Insist on this throughout the year. It is just one more example of how you can give structure to an environment that is too often unstructured. We have seen some rooms where each day the pupils' desks inch forward a little. After a few weeks, the teacher and her desk are backed up against the front chalkboard.

Overprepare lessons for the first day. It is better to have too much material in the lesson plans for the first few days than too little. Make the first day of school a "real" day complete with homework. This will tell your pupils that you mean business. Prepare a dozen sharpened pencils in advance or have some ball point pens for the students who come unprepared. But tell the class that after this each pupil is responsible for providing his or her own tools.

By setting up your own seating plan with desk labels on the first day, you will have an edge on learning names. You can certainly change seats later on—especially if you want to separate some chatterboxes. But on "day one" you are in charge and this will avoid having pupils charge into the room and take any seat they want.

Put an agenda on the chalkboard. This will let the class know what to expect. Pupils don't like surprises when it comes to a new situation. It gives them a sense of security to have a "road map" the first few days. Make the first day's homework assignment fairly easy. This will make even the slowest pupils feel a sense of accomplishment rather than frustration. But emphasize that homework will be checked carefully. And, as with everything you say to your class, follow through the next day. Give authority to what you say by keeping every promise.

examples of opening remarks that establish your authority

In addition to what you say, you must phrase your message in such a way that it carries extra punch. After listening to hundreds of teachers issue commands, we have concluded that short, terse commands are best. A simple, "You, come here!" is infinitely better than, "The boy in the blue shirt, get up and come to the front of the room, please."

Remember, at the beginning of the term you want to establish your authority. The best way to do it is by making sure your pupils understand you. The best way to do that is to speak in short, clear sentences or phrases. Pupils have a way of shutting their ears when a teacher gets involved in long sentences. Try to develop a "telegram" approach to instructions and directions. This will not be great prose but it will get your message across. After you are confident that you are in command, you can embellish your sentences with adjectives and adverbs.

During the first few days, do not be afraid to begin most of your sentences with: "You will . . ." This has a hypnotic effect after repetition and your pupils begin to silently respond with "I will." This may sound a little dogmatic at first. We know that when you took courses at the university they never told you to do this. But then again, they probably never taught a class quite like yours, either. After you have established your authority, you can ease up and become more relaxed and natural in your delivery. However, those first few days are critical. This can't be stressed enough. The attitudes that your pupils develop about you that first week are hard to change. You must be the authority figure or else the best-written lesson plans will fall on deaf ears for the rest of the year. The wise teacher will avoid the breeding ground of discontent by establishing control right from the start.

Another trick is to use nonverbal communication whenever possible. For example, a pupil may ask, "Where do we put the papers when we are finished?" Instead of telling him and thus disturbing the pupils who are still writing, merely point to the spot where you want the papers to be placed. Be sure to make eye contact as you point. By riveting your eyes on his you are reinforcing your silent command as you point.

In your opening remarks, be sure to mention some of the special things that you have planned for the term, such as a trip. This will give your youngsters something to look forward to. Of course, with a difficult class you can add a postscript like: ". . . only those pupils who have behaved well will be going."

While making your opening remarks, you can further establish your authority by walking around the room. This will necessitate having the pupils turn to see you as you approach their desks. This is another trick that shows them who is boss. Also, by walking around the room you can pause at the desk of a pupil who appears to be inattentive. Having you stand in front of his desk for a minute or two while you speak is guaranteed to wake him up from his daydream or get his eyes away from the open window. (Our use of the masculine pronoun is merely for convenience. As an experienced teacher you know that girls can be just as distracted as boys.)

Perhaps the best way to give your opening remarks even more clout is to talk very softly. The greatest compliment I ever received from a pupil whom other teachers could not handle was, "Mr. Chernow hollers *low*." I did not "holler" at all, but by talking softly and insisting on compliance with my deadly stare, I made him feel that he was being "hollered at" and he responded positively. Your pupils will have to stop their own whispering to hear you if you drop your voice when you are telling them something they want to hear— for example, when they go to gym. After a while, they will remain quiet to hear everything you have to say. On those rare occasions when you *do* raise your voice, it will have twice as much impact because of the low tones you use 90 percent of the time.

ways to handle that first morning

Set your alarm a half-hour earlier that first morning. Make sure you get to school early so that you can become aware of any last minute changes the administration may have made. The extra minutes may afford you time to go over your plans or check to see if you have enough books for each pupil. You will then be able to enjoy a few minutes in which to relax before you greet your new class. This is also a good time to hold a brief conversation with yourself in which you reinforce your objectives for the new year.

1. I will establish good control from the very beginning.
2. I will not become seduced into relaxing my guard and becoming a "pal."
3. I will establish good work habits in my pupils first and worry about content later.

Be in your room when your pupils arrive. This is imperative if you want to establish order in your classroom. We recommend that you stand just outside your classroom door and insist on a straight line before you let the first child enter. In some schools you will be picking the class up from a central area. In other schools the pupils will go to their rooms on their own. In either case, do not let any children enter the room until you have determined that they are ready to enter your domain. Psychologically, this establishes the fact that you are in control. It is your "turf" they are about to tread on. It is not a new area that they are going to take over or annex. Do not do a lot of talking while you are waiting. A silent stare accompanied by a raised finger will get your message across. After a few seconds, announce that the girls will go in first. This further reminds the pupils that you care about how they come into the room. If you can't do this the very first day of school, you are unlikely to get it done at a later date. So, take a few extra minutes and get it done properly. If, for some reason understandable to your class, you do not like the way the class came into the room, tell them that they must do it again. Line them up in the hall and start over. The extra five minutes will be well-spent.

On the first day, the pupils will line up on opposite sides of the room waiting to be seated. You have put their names on their desks ahead of time. But you don't want them rushing in and running from seat to seat looking for their names. When the two lines inside the room are quiet, you may call one name at a time and that pupil will be seated. This is a great way for you to make the association between the name and the face.

Have your name on the chalkboard. Unless your name is fairly easy to read, like Smith or Jones, pronounce it for them. Also point out how it is spelled and whether you prefer Miss, Ms., Mrs., Mr. or Dr.

Go through a similar ritual for hanging up outer clothing. Right after that, insist that pupils get busy with some written work. This can be a diagnostic test, a rexographed work sheet, or work from the board. It is not too soon to show your pupils that their main activity this year is going to be work and not play or horseplay. Do not allow any child to get up and sharpen a pencil or ask some extraneous question. All that can wait the 15 minutes that this assignment will take. While they are busy, you can "check them out" visually. Do not use this time to bury your nose in a roll book or desk drawer. This is the testing period and you must come through with flying colors.

how to develop a command presence

If you have done what we have suggested in the last few pages, you are on your way to developing a command presence. Our observation of thousands of teachers underscores the fact that you don't have to be tall, muscular, or long-limbed to convey a "take-charge" image to your pupils. We have all seen small, frail, elderly teachers exert a strong, positive, controlling influence on their classes while the former football tackle in the room next door has his class walking all over him.

Here are some hints that will help you gain the immediate respect of your class.

Speak in short sentences with emphasis on the verbs of each of your commands. For example: "You will *walk* to the end of the hall." This erases from the pupils' minds any images they may have had of running, sliding, or pushing.

Stand up to your full height even if some of your pupils are taller than you are. This will make you feel tall and in command even if you measure 4'11" wearing high heels.

Become as omnipresent as any mortal can. The pupils must sense your presence everywhere. Do not become a prisoner locked behind a desk. Walk around the room as you speak. Occasionally stand in the rear of the room as you give directions for seat or board work. You will get a different perspective from that vantage point. Also, the pupils seated in the rear will sense your control. Be sure to sit in the seat of an absent pupil from time to time. This will wake up the pupils on either side. Or, if they are sufficiently awake, perhaps hyperactive, your presence will serve as a sedative.

Use your eyes as well as your voice. When you issue a command, do not look at the floor or a spot on the wall. Focus your eyes directly on the eyes of the pupil you are addressing. When speaking to the whole class, move your eyes from face to face. Successful teachers can describe the shape and color of the eyes of every difficult pupil in their class. After doing this for a while they find they have fewer difficult pupils.

Use the "Tower of Pisa" approach. When talking to an individual pupil about some misbehavior, *lean* toward him. Physical proximity is an important "law enforcement" weapon. If you do it right, you will never have to touch a child and yet he or she will feel restrained. Never fold your arms across your chest while admonishing a pupil. This is a self-protective gesture and is read as a sign of weakness.

Don't turn your back too soon on a situation. Let's say two pupils are arguing at their seats. You follow all of the above suggestions and tell the students, "Back to work . . . NOW!" This is not enough. You must stand there and make sure that they have indeed gone back to their work before you turn your back and move away. The extra minute or two you spend at the scene of the crime will prevent a reoccurrence. To show that you always have the last word, after they have been back to work for two minutes, or thereabouts, say in a loud, clear voice, "That's better," or simply, "Good." This will show the rest of the class that the teacher "won" again.

Practice these suggestions every day and they will become second nature to you. They will also lead you into little tricks of your own. Those are always the best. Before you know it, you will feel that you are in command; the pupils will sense your presence and respect it. "Nothing succeeds like success." Once you have succeeded in improving classroom discipline in one area, it will spill over into another area. In the eyes of your pupils you will be surrounded by an aura of respect.

how to establish productive routines

Once you have gotten through the first day, you must work hard at establishing routines. Pupils need specific ways of doing things whether it's a format for heading their written work or a plan for giving out supplementary books. Sometimes it will seem easier if you let the pupils do some routine tasks as they please. You might rationalize, "Why not let them do it *their* way? Why not save the commands for really important matters?" Nothing could be further from the truth! It is not easier to let pupils do as they wish. It may seem easier at first. But you can be sure that, after a day or two of this, your class will "take over" in every way. You must not abdicate your position of leadership. Don't think of waiting for the "important" things to establish routines; important arrangements are just the sum of a lot of little routines.

Productive routines are an outgrowth of setting standards. Half-hearted teaching, careless work, sloppy notebooks and poor behavior come from teaching without standards. You must set standards for yourself if you expect your pupils to meet certain requirements of yours.

Be consistent. Don't insist on certain routines for sharpening pencils today and then ignore them all of next week. Routines are not merely a fetish of a neurotic teacher; they have a sound rationale. Routines save time, they give pupils a sense of security, they are efficient ways of doing things, and they have survived "trial and error" testing. Brain surgeons follow certain routines when they operate. Major crimes are solved by police routines and procedures. An orderly classroom where learning can take place is insured with routines.

how to survive the pupils' testing period

No matter how carefully you study this book and implement its points, your class is going to test you for the first few days. You can survive the pupils' testing period if you are determined. Remember, you are older and more experienced than they are. This should make up for their strength in numbers. They are going to be on the lookout for your weakest area—your Achilles' heel. Do you let things slide after lunch? Is Friday the day when you let almost anything go? Do you show favoritism and let some kids get away with murder? All of these are "no-no's." You have to come across as firm but *fair*. All of the pupils must feel that you stick by your rules and insist that *everyone* follow them.

Start slowly in establishing yourself as the supreme commander. Don't overwhelm the class with 99 rules on the first day followed by another two dozen every day thereafter. A steady well-organized pace is far better than a big extravaganza that fizzles out. Remember to act calm; nervousness, fear, and frustration are highly contagious. If you are infected with any of these "germs" you are sure to spread it around the classroom. Stick it out. Just when you feel that you are getting nowhere, a light will shine at the end of the tunnel. The first two weeks are tough. But if you start out right and stick to your guns, the rest of the term will be smooth sailing. Gain control early to avoid an uphill struggle later on. It is far easier to relax control than it is to impose it once it has been lost.

During the testing period, try to give compliments as well as scolding or correcting pupils. A cheerful "Henry knows what to do" will get other children to see what is so great about Henry's behavior and they will consciously or unconsciously copy it. Don't be afraid to compliment a pupil whom you have had to discipline a few minutes earlier. This will make him feel that you are unhappy with what he did and not with him as a person. This is very important. Your pupils must feel that you like them even though you sometimes do not like what they are doing.

tips on improving the physical environment

Sometime after the classes in your building have been dismissed, take a walk down the hall and stop to look into various classrooms. You will notice that well-controlled, orderly classes live in orderly classrooms. If your school has one or two disorderly classes, you will notice that the rooms they live in all day are also chaotic and disorganized. A disarranged room has a tendency to make children disorderly, too. Your first step is to arrange the furniture to give maximum use of space. There should be provision made for the orderly movement of pupils as they hang their clothing, get books, use interest centers, etc. They should be able to do this without climbing over materials or each other.

Your room should give life to the catchword "a place for everything and everything in its place." Insist that books be returned to shelves when not being used. Paintbrushes, science materials and other messy materials must be washed before being put away. By insisting on good housekeeping rules you will be furthering a sense of self-discipline. At the same time, you will be giving your pupils a sense of pride in where they live. Let's face it, as an adult, where are you more likely to toss a gum wrapper if no litter cans exist—on an already refuse-strewn street or on one that is clean and well cared for?

Make every pupil an integral part of your classroom. Be sure you have some piece of work up on a bulletin board from every child in the room. If it is not a test paper, it may be a picture or cartoon, just as long as it has his or her name on it. It may even be a child's initials formed into a monogram of his own design and colored with crayons. Each child should feel that part of him is on display and that he is part of this class.

Place your desk in a prominent place. The children should feel that the teacher is important and that is why she can see everyone from her seat. If you shove your desk into a corner you will be giving your pupils quite a different message. Feel free to change certain pupils' seats so that they are near you. Proximity to the teacher often prevents problems. The way in which you arrange your pupils' furniture sends nonverbal messages from you to them. There is no best floor plan for every classroom; if there were we would print it on the cover of this book. If you want an absolutely quiet room and teach a group that needs structure and direction, you will want to have a more rigid arrangement of furniture. For example, all children face the teacher, the teacher's desk is in front of the room, no two pupils' desks touch one another.

If you are comfortable with some group work and some pupil socialization, you may arrange your room with your desk off to the side of the room and pairs of pupils' desks lined up together. Later in the term you may feel your class is ready for committee work and your room might set up with clusters of six or eight pupils' desks touching one another. You, the teacher, must be comfortable with the setup.

The behavior in your room will, to a large extent, be determined by the environment you create. Begin with an arrangement of furniture that will meet your needs as well as theirs.

how to set up limits that help pupils behave better

Imagine, if you will, a crowded deck of passengers on board a luxury liner. One end of the deck has a thick guardrail and one end of the deck has none. At which end of the deck are the passengers more comfortable? At which end is there more freedom of movement and less tension? The answer is obvious. In a like manner, children who have clearly defined limits established early in the term possess the same sense of security as the passengers with the guardrail. They know they can go just so far and no further. They know that the rail is for their own protection. The rail even helps them get closer to the edge without a fear of falling off. You must set these limits for your class. Experience has proven that children can't set them for themselves. In some rare cases, the children, together with their teacher, can draw up a list of limits. But they can never establish limits on their own. Did you ever see a school child agreeing with his parents about bedtime at bedtime? However, if 9:00 P.M. was established earlier and the youngster knows that his parents mean business, there is no quibbling at 9:00 P.M.

A good way to establish limits is to have them listed on a bulletin board in the room. Another way is to have pupils write them in their notebooks. Here are some simple, but effective, limits we have collected from different classrooms:

1. No one leaves the room before 9:30 A.M.
2. Only two pencils may be sharpened at one time.
3. No talking during a fire drill.
4. Pupils who were absent must bring a note from home when they return to school.
5. All talking stops when the teacher raises her hand.
6. Children may not wear hats indoors.

There are a variety of ways to enforce these rules. But first you must review them with your class. Also, explain the reason for each rule. Better still, ask your pupils to give the reason for each rule. This will give you a great deal of insight into their thinking.

One way to enforce the rules is to refer to them when they are broken. For example, "John, go to the board and read Rule #3."

Or, you can rexograph the list of rules and circle the rule that a youngster violated. This sheet is then sent home and the parent is asked to sign the sheet.

A child needs to feel that someone is in control and is responsible for his environment. The opposite is also true; if he senses that no one is setting limits, he is apt to lose control of himself. Children need to feel that someone not only sets limits but also maintains them. Hyperactive or disturbed children fear their own powers of destructiveness and really want someone to maintain limits.

In setting limits you must also separate the way children *feel* from the way that they *act*. "I can understand how you felt when Duane took your ball; you had a right to be angry. But kicking him was the wrong thing to do. Do you see that now?" Notice how the teacher acknowledged "bad" or "angry" feelings? She drew the limit though when it came to acting out that feeling. This skilled teacher added a tag line: "Do you see that now?" This is a face-saver for the child. She is really saying: "If you didn't do the right thing before, do you at least understand what I would expect of you next time?"

Try to identify the kind of behavior that bothers you. Knowing what bothers one teacher may be important to another. A reading teacher might be upset by insubordination, but the gym teacher may not worry about it. So the pupil gets mixed messages as to what kinds of behaviors are important.

In conclusion, the most important thing about a system of setting limits or any other discipline system is that people have the feeling that something is being done. Just by having you write out a referral card or make a note in your "red book," a pupil sees that something is going to happen. Parents should know that action is being taken in school by means of a note home, a phone call, or a notation in the pupil's homework book. Teachers must let administrators know what steps have already been taken. There should be a pervading feeling that things are being dealt with in a fair way.

2

handling
specific discipline
infractions

In the first chapter we showed you how to set the tone for the school year, starting with "day number one." There are certain common types of behavior problems that manifest themselves in virtually every classroom: fighting, stealing, foul language, hyperactivity, cheating, etc. While these specific discipline problems occur in every school level, in every state of the union, there are some antidotes and preventive steps that you can take.

what to do about constant talkers

This variety of troublemaker is equally likely to be a boy or girl. For some children, talking appears to be a nervous habit—they just can't help chattering. For others it's an attempt at getting the teacher's "goat" either consciously or unconsciously. Whatever the reason, you can put a stop to talking by trying these tested and proven techniques:

1. Keep a "limbo" chair near your desk. This is a seat that is kept vacant on most days and is not assigned to any one pupil. On a day when Helen or Jim cannot stop talking, assign the chatterer to this "limbo" seat. You can now keep a closer watch and the talker is away from his avid listener.

2. Ask questions so that the talker is forced to pay attention. For example, ". . . what do you think about that, Jim?" Avoid sarcasm and don't show your annoyance. To do so would indicate that the pupil was successful in getting your "goat."

3. Use the "icy stare" technique. This will freeze some talkers into silence. It is especially effective if you stop talking in the middle of a sentence and just rivet your eyes on the talker. Avoid this method for the very brazen who would just enjoy the attention paid by the rest of the class.

4. Offer a choice of punishment to the serious offender mentioned above. Something like: "Which do you prefer, Helen, a written assignment or staying after school?" This tells the whole class that the teacher means business. Our interviews with hundreds of pupils have revealed that they much prefer the teacher who "does something" to the one who "just lectures or screams." They admitted that making them "do" something was more likely to get them to stop than any amount of talk.

5. Appeal to their "macho" or "femme" instincts. Say something like, "Jim, you don't realize how far your deep, masculine voice carries." Or, "Helen, your sultry voice can be heard by every boy in this room." Of course, you must gear your remarks to the age level of your pupils.

6. Use nonverbal communication. Just stroll over to the offender while continuing your lesson and move his or her chair out of line slightly. Do this without stopping your lesson. The offender will get the point and the attention he or she craves without losing face.

These tricks will work with the mildly incorrigible. You will need different techniques for the really hostile, acting-out pupil.

how to handle the openly defiant pupil

The first thing you must remember is that *you* are not the target. It may seem that the youngster hates you, but in reality you are not the target of his rage; you are merely the person available to him. His parents may have had a fight at the breakfast table. His family may be moving again. He or she may be physically ill and not aware of it. A whole host of emotional problems may be surfacing.

Whatever the cause, you MUST do something about such outbursts if you are to have the respect of the rest of the class and if you are to be of any help to the offender. Don't fall into the trap of taking such behavior personally. When a teacher takes this defiant behavior s something directed at herself she begins to lose her effectiveness. Here are some ways of handling the problem.

1. If possible, ignore the first outburst. If the offender sees that you are not easily riled he may drop this tactic and just quiet down.

2. At the second offense, or if the first one is not something you can ignore, isolate the pupil. Use an empty chair near you or a seat in the rear. For more serious offenses send him to the office with a note of explanation. For young children, send another, more responsible, pupil with him.

3. Open your marking book and make a notation. This may be a phrase or just some doodle on your part; make sure the pupil and class see that you are "recording" his misbehavior.

4. Keep the rest of the class working, preferably at something that does not require your attention. Use this time to speak to the defiant pupil in the hall or at your desk.

5. Insist calmly but firmly that the nonsense be stopped.

6. If misbehavior stops quickly, continue the lesson as if nothing has happened.

7. Later on, determine the cause: work too difficult, physical indisposition, emotional reaction, lack of motivation, etc. Follow up as needed.

8. The child who has lost control must be dealt with immediately.

We hope these outbursts will become fewer in number as you master these techniques. Remember this; the best disciplinarian in your school was not born that way. It is by trial and error that successful techniques are learned. We have done some of the dirty work for you by singling out the best methods that have worked for master teachers on every school level. Good disciplinarians are made! Follow these suggestions and *you* will have it made! Remember this: competent, take-charge teachers come in all sizes, shapes, and colors. The common thread running through all such good teachers is a sense of confidence in themselves and a huge bag of tricks that they have acquired through the years. We will fill your bag of tricks in the time it takes you to read this book. You will then develop that sense of confidence.

And that is not cheating. It is merely taking the short cut to mastery of your chosen profession. Let's talk about pupils who do cheat.

four things you can do about cheating

1. Reduce or prevent cheating on tests by taking the pressure off your pupils. Try to show them by word and deed that you respect them as people and not according to their test scores. Indicate that most tests are for your benefit; they show you how many of the pupils learned the material you taught. Encourage pupils to compete only with themselves. They should not compare their scores with those of other pupils. They should be interested in seeing how they do in comparison to their last test.

2. When you discover that a child has cheated by copying someone else's homework, looked at another pupil's test paper, peeked at a book or notes during an exam, or done some other dishonest act, emphasize the behavior and not the pupil. Show them that it is the action you disapprove of and not the pupil. Stress that the pupil is cheating himself and not the teacher.

3. Don't embarrass or humiliate the pupil. Don't call attention to the cheating in front of the whole class. There is nothing to be gained by having the pupil lose face before his peers. Your talking to him or her after class will be humiliating enough.

4. After you have spoken to the cheater, treat the issue as closed. Act toward the offender as you do toward other pupils. In most cases the lesson will have been learned and there is no point in reliving it.

Just as in all life situations, you as the adult should aviod putting temptation in the path of youngsters. For example, don't step out of the room during a test. This is likely to test the honesty of virtually every pupil.

how to handle pupils who refuse to do any work

The avoidance of a confrontation with the youngster while rewarding cooperative behavior is the basic key to success with pupils who refuse to work. Here are some things you can do:

1. Focus on the situations where the pupil shows an interest. Praise him for the work he does in science, art, physical education or some other favorite subject.

2. Ignore in a very matter-of-fact way any confrontations with the pupil. The negativistic child has discovered that negativism very often is a sure way to gain attention.

3. Reduce your criteria for the correctness of a task while you're working with his refusal to do work. Reduce expectations. Settle for small gains and resist constant preoccupation with success.

4. Such pupils are supersensitive to any perceived unfairness by the teacher. Favored treatment of others, real or imagined, leads these children to sulk, brood, and do no work. Be very careful to treat all "refuse-niks" in the same way. Class discussions of fairness can help reduce angry, hostile feelings.

5. Give your pupils a feeling of success through assignment of reasonable tasks and your personal encouragement. Show that you appreciate their efforts and abilities.

ways to get the hyperactive pupil to settle down

There are some children who just can't settle down. Some of these have been diagnosed by school psychologists as hyperactive.

"His mind is like a TV set on which someone is always changing the channels." That is the way one Bureau of Child Guidance psychologist described Natan. Like a TV set, he is the receiver of rapidly changing signals over which he has little control. In the classroom it is impossible for him to complete a task, to organize activities, to work independently, or even to sit still for more than five minutes.

If you have had such a child, or children, in your classroom, then you know how demanding it is to teach hyperactive children and at the same time maintain a semblance of order in the room. Here are some classroom management strategies that we have tested:

1. Provide as much structure as you can. Make classroom rules and procedures consistent from day to day. These children do not like surprises.

2. Minimize distractions. The hyperactive child is very sensitive to all kinds of stimuli. Avoid seating him or her in the middle or back of the room. Keep such a child away from the window.

3. Couple verbal messages with visual clues to reinforce a message. For example, if you want the child to work silently, place your index finger on your lips. If you want him to get his math workbook out of his desk, hold up a copy of yours.

4. Slip a sheet of brightly-colored construction paper underneath the child's paper to help him or her focus attention on the assignment.

5. Set up a quiet corner somewhere in the room where this child can go during brief periods throughout the day. You may be able to move a bookcase and easel to form a small "office" on the side of the room.

As the term progresses, offer the child choices whenever feasible. For example, instead of telling him or her to stop working on the drawing, propose an activity that's more acceptable to you. Being able to make a choice can be very important to hyperactive children; it gives them a chance to exert some control over what they do.

Keep notes on the student's behavior and relay them to the guidance counselor or school psychologist. This kind of information on the child's functioning is of great value to the clinician or physician treating the pupil.

what to do about pupils who use foul language

In recent years, different standards have been drawn up as far as what is and what is not acceptable language. If you're working with children whose cultural background permits greater lenience in language standards than your own, be sensitive in your consideration of the youngsters' loyalty to their peers. In some communities you may want to explain that there is "street" talk and "school" talk.

Here are several suggestions that were contributed by teachers who "draw the line when it comes to certain words."

1. Indicate calmly that the language used is improper for your classroom and uncalled for. Explain that in your classroom you accept and expect the same language that is acceptable in your home.

2. If the remark is just an isolated outburst of temper, keep your own record but try to adjust the matter by talking to the pupil in private.

3. Don't insist on a public apology. If the pupil is truly repentant, his attitude will be evident to the entire class.

4. Don't take obscenity as a personal affront but as an offense against the class and the school.

5. For older pupils, suggest that, instead of swearing, they invent two or three personal expletives and use these to let off steam (e.g. fishcakes, shingle, drain).

6. One final bit of advice: all of us learn language by parroting others. Foul language is just as contagious as slang. If the children who swear are not pressured to stop, other children who formerly didn't swear will start it. Don't abdicate your responsibility by turning a deaf ear. Your pupils will respect you more if you insist on a standard of decency. You might try to include the class in setting up such a standard. You can always steer the discussion by asking them if they ever heard such language on TV or radio.

Worse yet than the youngster who is cussin' and fussin' is the one who steals!

six ways you can prevent stealing

The best way to prevent stealing is to build an atmosphere of trust. If pupils feel that you trust them they will act in a trustworthy manner. If they feel that you are always suspicious of them, they will give you cause to be suspicious.

As in cheating or other offenses, don't tempt your pupils. The teacher who leaves her handbag or wallet unattended is asking for trouble. It is unfair to expect a group of pupils to resist such temptation.

If something of value is missing, give the culprit a chance to return the article immediately without penalty. Designate an empty desk or wastebasket where the missing item can be returned before dismissal time. Often the missing item will miraculously reappear when you promise amnesty.

If the article is not returned and you find the culprit, send a referral form at once. Theft, as distinct from mere mischief, is a serious offense. If you do not do something about it, it will spread like wildfire. If the article is not returned or discovered, send promptly for a school official. Keep the class in the room until the assistant principal or other official arrives. If you allow anyone to leave the room, even to go to the bathroom, it is unlikely that the owner of the missing property will ever see it again.

After you have corrected a stealing incident, take an early opportunity to show the child that you trust him. Have him carry money in an envelope to the office, for example—if you feel he has learned his lesson.

You can prevent stealing of school property by setting up a "lending system." Very often a child is momentarily enticed into stealing something and then tires of it quickly. At this point, he has a problem. If he tries to return it to school, he may get caught. If he keeps it at home, his mother may ask questions. The safest course, too often, is to ditch it in some waste can or dark alley. Then everyone loses. Under the lending system, any portable object in the room may be checked out for a weekend. This includes athletic equipment, metric measures, art supplies, science materials.

One teacher we know has been making an offer that everyone refuses. She tells her pupils she doesn't want to see them tempted. She asks that they let her know if there's any small item in the room they want so much that they might be tempted to take it. She tells them that she'll give it to them. The children are baffled by her offer—she doesn't have any stealing, either. It's no fun taking something that you could have had for the asking.

A traditional method for getting back a stolen item is to detain the whole class after school until the purloined item is returned. This puts some peer pressure on the pupil who stole the item. If this does not work, you can add an additional step. Explain to the class that it isn't fair to let the guilty party go scot-free. Hand out a sheet of paper to each pupil. Instruct them to write one of two messages on the piece of paper: "I didn't take it." or "I took it and I'm sorry." Each pupil signs his paper, folds it, and places it on the teacher's desk. The teacher's part of the pact is to let the offender remain anonymous that day, and to settle with him or her later. Sometimes, just returning the merchandise is punishment enough. You wouldn't want to punish the whole class for the actions of one pupil unless all other methods have failed.

how to reduce fighting between pupils

"Some children do not know when they are fighting." This surprising statement was made by a senior teacher who weighs about 98 pounds yet controls a difficult class in an inner city school. In her pupils' minds, wrestling and pummeling your buddy is not fighting. "After all, the other guy is having fun, too," her youngsters are likely to say.

Sometimes such scrapping is merely a habit. Often, it reflects home standards. Many working-class parents teach their boys to fight, and are proud of the youngster who "can lick every kid on the block." Many girls are just as proficient as the boys. Physical force is a way of life in poorer areas. But, even "fun fighting" can change over into real bitterness in a matter of seconds. That's when the teacher has to be watchful. She could have a very ugly situation on her hands if she is not careful. Talking things over with the combatant's parents is a "must" if this has happened more than once.

Escort the fighter to the office and dial his home or the parent's work number. When you get his mother on the line, explain that there has been another fight. At this point, put Junior on the phone. Let him tell her the whole story. You stand next to him as he talks. This way the parent gets the story straight from the "horse's mouth." Also, it gives the mother time, before her son arrives home, to think over how she wants to handle the incident.

When a fight breaks out, separate the two pupils at once. Speak firmly and briefly. Do not take sides at this point. Let the certainty of your voice inform them that there is definite outside, adult control. This is not the time to reason with them about their fighting. In a few minutes you will notice changed facial expressions. Feelings will have calmed by now. This is the time to talk to each child separately. In a relaxed, friendly voice explain your earlier abruptness and tell them you'd always rather talk and reason with pupils. Your relaxed manner will quiet them even more.

One special kind of fighting involves the bully. Every bully has a story. Usually his life has been troubled in some way. This is his way of getting even and making himself feel better. But you as the teacher cannot allow it. Some of your shyest pupils will be afraid that "Ralph will get me after school."

If this is the case, when you dismiss your class, leave the bully in the room while you walk the other youngsters to the dismissal door. By the time you return to the room, two or three minutes will have passed. This is long enough for a child to be left alone in an empty classroom to think. Let him go with a warning that if any harm befalls the shy pupil you will hold him responsible. A word to the wise is usually sufficient.

If there has been a fight which you are quite sure was unprovoked by the loser, have the bully-winner meet the loser's parents for a conference. This is a great way to get through the tough exterior that some youngsters display. Clear this conference, in advance, with your principal.

Should the argument continue after class or after school, arrange for both sets of parents to get together.

a case history

Robert looks as if he might be a choir boy. His blond hair and large blue eyes would never indicate that his cumulative record card contains entries that read in part: *incorrigible, uncontrollable temper, impulsive behavior, shows sadistic tendencies, always fighting.*

Robert is somewhat shorter than the other pupils in his class, but he is sturdily built and quite capable of handling himself with older, bigger boys. His achievement test scores indicate that he is quite capable of doing the work of his grade, yet he seldom comes prepared and shows no interest in his schoolwork.

At his teacher's request, Robert's parents took him to the family physician for a complete physical checkup. The doctor found nothing organically wrong and eliminated the possibility of any neurological impairment.

Mr. Dicke, Robert's teacher, kept him in the classroom during lunch one day because of disruptive behavior in the lunchroom the day before. While both were eating, Mr Dicke asked Robert if he had a nickname. Robert blushed and said the other kids called him

"PeeWee." Mr. Dicke asked him how he felt about that and Robert replied that he "hated it."

This opened a door into Robert's troubled ego. Further talks revealed that this boy was preoccupied with his "shortness" and was reacting to his exaggerated perception of himself.

Mr. Dicke told him about his own troubled childhood because he was the "skinniest" kid in his class and couldn't compete in competitive sports. Other discussions centered around the meaninglessness of nicknames. At another lunch conference, Robert was named "Bobby" by Mr. Dicke and, after that, whenever he was called "PeeWee" in the schoolyard he quickly responded with, "My name is Bobby."

Not every story has such a happy ending. And don't think that Bobby never got into scraps after this. But much of his hostility was diminished because he was less angry. The point we are trying to make is that the most miserable child in your class is that way for a reason. Don't give up trying to discover the reasons for anti-social behavior.

3

managing group discipline problems

It's one thing to be able to reach out and handle one or two discipline problems in your class. But some of us are not so lucky—we have whole classes of pupils with behavior problems. How do we control such a group? First, by telling ourselves that we can! There is a tremendous element of psychological dominance required of teachers in today's schools. Unless you walk into the room each day confident that you will be in control, that you are the captain of your ship, you are in for trouble. As young as they are, your pupils can sense any weakness or hesitancy you display.

In this chapter we are going to give you practical solutions to problems that a whole class might present. Let's begin by taking a look at how you can improve class conduct when you are out of the room with your crew.

ways to handle your class in out-of-classroom settings

Mrs. Reese has high standards for pupil behavior in her classroom and her pupils seem to know how to go to the gym or the school library without pushing, running, or butting one another. The teacher across the hall has trouble controlling her children in the room and when they go to recess it resembles a stampede of cattle. Are these exceptions? Certainly not! There is a positive correlation between classroom and out-of-classroom behavior. Don't slacken your efforts to maintain good order with your class when out of the room. Bad habits will just come back to haunt you when you return to the classroom.

Let's begin with movement in the hall. There are many occasions when you want the class to go from your room to another place: fire drills, lunch, recess, assemblies, special subject areas, etc. Quiet movement begins IN the classroom. Don't be rushed. If you are late, the class will sense it and act up. Anticipate when and where you are going. Get the class ready by having them put their work away. This simple gesture will get them set for going on to the next location. If you merely tell them, "Stop work, leave everything on your desk and line up," you are confusing them. It is better to say: "Stop work and put everything away." After a minute or two, add: "Boys—on line; (pause) girls—on line."

Notice the difference in the two commands. In the first one you are inviting confusion. When you tell the pupils to leave their work on their desks some will take a minute longer to finish. Others will look at a neighbor's work; still others will look for a pencil to swipe. With the second command, the pupils are told to put everything away. This provides a natural completion to one activity and a psychological readiness for a new activity—getting on line. Notice that the boys were invited to line up first. This should be alternated from time to time. The important point is to have half the class getting out of their seats at one time, instead of the whole class.

We are now ready to leave the classroom and proceed to the new location (gym, science room, library, etc.) The first pair of pupils is told, "Go down to the swinging door (or clock, or fire extinguisher)." The important thing is that the first pair of pupils is directed to move out of the room and move to a fixed point, with the rest of the class following. This allows you, the teacher, to oversee how everyone leaves the room. A glassy stare will keep the "wise guys" from trying anything "funny." This also allows you time to shut the lights, lock the door, and hurry the stragglers. You can then "review your troops" as they stand on line. It also gives you a chance to now get to the front of the line, if you wish. Or, you can continue your vigil from the rear of the line as you instruct the leaders to walk on to the staircase or another fixed point. The idea we are trying to convey is that you are "in charge" every minute as opposed to the weak teacher who just says, "Charge!" You decide if you want to insist on perfect silence as you go through the halls or if you want to allow quiet conversation.

Think through the sequence of events when you are out of the room with your class. For example, Miss Blois noticed that when her class went to the bathroom as a group, after outdoor recess, it took as long as 15 minutes. She reversed the sequence; the pupils went to the bathroom and THEN went outside for free play. Somehow, knowing they were on their way outside shortened their bathroom stay by two-thirds.

how to develop a sense of cooperation

Each of your pupils is an individual. In college you learned all about individual differences and the need to individualize instruction. But in the realities of the classroom there are times when you want to merge all these diverse personalities into one cohesive group. Only by developing this sense of community or group can you reduce group tensions and help your pupils learn to live in a civilized, caring society.

Every football coach knows how to fire up his team. It will pay for you to take a lesson from the coach and get your pupils to think of themselves as a unit. We are not endorsing strong competitive pep talks. These might backfire—when your kids beat up the kids from across the hall. But rather, we urge that you instill in your class a sense of pride in their group. This is easier to do than you might expect. Children have a strong sense of loyalty to their family, neighborhood, club, or block association. Capitalize on that and you will have less trouble getting their attention and teaching lessons to the whole class.

Children of all ages love secrets and "code words." Why not ask them to select a secret word that only the pupils in your class will know. It might be an ethnic word if most of your class belongs to one group; an African, Hispanic, or Italian word. This code word then becomes a synonym for "cooperation." It might even be a nonsense word like, "ajocco." When something comes up in class where you would like to see some collective effort, for example, at clean-up time, just ask the pupils to use a little "ajocco." You will be amazed at the wry smiles and busy hands that such a request will bring.

Why a secret word? Kids are tired of admonitions about cooperation. A new word, a secret word, makes it possible for them to develop a more complex image of collective work and mutual respect. The following illustrates this.

In one fourth-grade class there was only one pupil who knew how to play chess. When his teacher encouraged him to teach the others to play, he said he didn't want to teach someone else how to beat him. By appealing to his "ajocco" his teacher was able to get him to share his expertise. After six weeks the whole class was able to play. The original player's ego was assuaged because instead of calling it "chess" that class alone called it "Brian's Game," after him.

After you have developed a sense of cooperation you will be ready to focus on self-discipline.

five ways to promote self-discipline

1. Build a good relationship. If you want your kids to become responsible for their own actions, you must build an attitude of mutual respect. You must be kind and firm. Firmness without a touch of kindness is not the answer. Your pupils must feel that you like them. Assure them that it is because of your concern for their welfare that you insist on certain things (safety rules, no running in the hall, orderly lineups, etc.).

2. Use logical consequences. Distinguish in word and deed the difference between "punishment" and "logical consequences." Punishment demands compliance with rules. Punishment conveys the threat of disrespect or loss of love. Logical consequences give the pupil a choice: "If I do this and the teacher finds out then I am sure to . . . " The logical consequence of stealing, talking out, cheating on a test, or whatever, are known to the child before he commits the action. What happens to him (phone call to parent, letter home, principal's office) is known ahead of time. If he is caught he must face the "logical consequence." In this way the pupil knows it is the act and not the person who must "face the music." The child is still accepted as a worthwhile person; the act is wrong and what follows is logical and fair.

3. Promote decision-making skills. Responsibility and decision-making are dependent upon each other. Most children feel that they make few decisions for themselves. Children who act out or disturbed

children feel even more strongly that they are often led to anti-social behavior. They rationalize away their own responsibilty for their behavior with: "You made me do it." Children need to feel that they are involved in the decision-making process. Point out to them how many decisions they make for themselves each day. This will enable them to realize that they *do* have choices in their daily lives; and, that they must bear the responsibilities for the choices they make.

4. Develop mutual respect. All of us at one time or another have identified with the comedian Rodney Dangerfield when he laments: "I don't get no respect." We wonder if he first had this feeling as a child in school! Very often the aggressive, disturbing pupil acts that way because respect for others has greatly diminished in our society and in our classrooms. Make your pupils understand that no one human being in your classroom is worth more than another. That means teachers respecting pupils, pupils respecting teachers, and hardest of all—pupils respecting each other. It must begin with you, the teacher. We hope it will transcend your classroom and reach out to the family, neighborhood, and society. Use encouragement constantly. Emphasize good parts of an assignment even if the whole paper isn't perfect. Hang up papers that are less than 100 percent. Give everyone of your pupils "a place in the sun." Recognize improvement and be lavish in your praise. Show trust and respect and belief in mutual respect; for example, "I'm sure you and Marie can settle this without further arguing. Let me know what you decide." If you have been encouraging, the reactions of your pupils will show it. They will begin to respect themselves and others more and more.

5. Have a responsible classroom. Set the tone for responsibility. Set up goals for the year, early. Put them down on a chart and post them on a bulletin board. Develop them with the pupils; add their ideas. Get their thinking on how the goals can be achieved. Refer to the "Code of Behavior" or set of rules throughout the year. This will keep the class aware of what each pupil is aiming for. Early in the year, have each pupil set his individual goals. Early in October hand out a sheet of paper and a legal size envelope. Ask each pupil to write down some specific behavior or work goals for himself for the year and sign the paper. These individual goals are then put in each pupil's envelope and collected; the envelope flaps are tucked in but not sealed. Two or three times throughout the year, hand out the envelopes and ask your pupils to evaluate their own progress.

These five methods of achieving self-discipline are based on mutual respect, self-responsibility, and better decision-making. Try them; you'll like them. And what's more, your children will like themselves better!

how to teach constructive criticism

In spite of your best efforts, your pupils will come up with complaints; complaints and criticism of you, their peers, the school, even their parents. Here are some tested approaches for dealing with them.

You must show your children suitable ways to protest against abuses (or what they perceive as abuses) of adult power. If you don't, they will just give you a hard time.

All pupils need safety valves. If they have no release, no voice, they develop a burdened feeling of resentment which is termed "oppression." Their reactions may take the form of apathy, hostility, or confrontation.

A preferred reaction is constructive criticism—a skill that can be learned. It's your job to show your pupils how to disagree with authority courteously, how to object intelligently. Disagreeing without letting tempers flare is a fine art, even for adults; it can start as early as first grade.

Begin by choosing a target topic. It must be debatable, it must be of universal concern, and it must be emotionally charged. For example, bedtime hour, weekend curfew, use of make-up or tobacco, dating, use of TV, etc. Structure a practice session using role-playing. Insist that pupils take turns taking parents' viewpoints and support them. Notice we have left out school-based topics like report cards or homework. In the beginning, let the children aim their arrows at a target other than the school or teacher. With practice you can lead them to protest school and class rules and procedures.

Another strategy is to invite pupils to write you a letter when they think some action on your part has been unfair. They may be shy at first. You may permit unsigned letters at the beginning of the term.

Keep a gripe box. It should be slotted so that notes can go in but cannot be removed by anyone other than the teacher. Any pupil who feels that something is amiss writes his comments and drops them in the box.

Encourage pupils to write down or discuss aloud the "perfect classroom" or "perfect teacher." The general atmosphere, kinds of freedom, teacher personality, and room appearance are all discussed. The class can think and talk about which ideas will work and why. It's amazing how many pupils recognize the need for courtesy and being soft-spoken—for everyone else, anyway.

a look at corporal punishment

Sometimes it's impossible to be soft-spoken. Something gets to us and we want to explode. Too often, we strike out.

Many reasons have been offered to explain the increased use of corporal punishment in the schools. It has been attributed to a variety of factors that have come to characterize much of the current scene: increasing violence in the cities and in the city schools; concern with law and order; pervasive doubts about the effectiveness of the school system; and gaps in the teacher's understanding of today's pupils. This increase, in spite of current laws and bylaws to the contrary, has been reported by national groups like the American Civil Liberties Union and the American Orthopsychiatric Association.

As children experience violence from the adults in their lives, they adopt this quality as a pattern to emulate. There is no question in our minds that hitting, whipping, slapping or striking pupils sets up a vicious cycle. When kids learn from their teachers that application of physical force by the controlling adult is an acceptable technique of management, they find little reason *not* to use this method as their own.

But what can you do when you feel they are "getting to you" and you are about to lose control? First, we might study ourselves. Take time to ask yourself what kinds of situations prompt you to explode.

Gather materials to deflect the rage of pupils and yourself— pillows to punch, scribbling and play equipment, puppets, etc.

Schedule and reschedule the curriculum to allow for active periods of play or gym after long periods of sitting or concentration for all pupils regardless of their grade level. This provides outlets of body tension for everyone.

Hold classroom discussions to discover which methods of control your pupils think work best for them. Why are they preferred? In this way the pupils play an active role in the development of classroom order.

Try to desensitize yourself to the usual, provoking four-letter words. Remember you are not the target of pupil rage most of the time.

Initiate a system of arranging trades with other teachers so that you are not punishing the same child all day long. A change of burdens is always comforting.

Institute a reward system for good days for the whole class. Make an effort to discover what causes the bad days.

These proposals, wisely incorporated into your planning and teaching, can help you more than you can imagine. Every teacher, even the most even-tempered member of your current staff, has felt the urge to strike a child. Some of us are better able to control that impulse. Let's face it; the pupils in our schools today are much more provocative than those in the past. But we as the professionals must keep control.

working with a whole class of "problem children"

Just think; there are teachers all over America who face each day with a roomful of difficult, attention-seeking, acting-out pupils. We know because we spoke to them and saw them in action. Here are some of their "secret weapons":

1. Keep your pupils as busy as you can. Find work that is relevant and easy enough for them to do. Provide a balance of short- and long-range projects.

2. Use competition, especially in the area of physical education. You don't have to be smart or rich to excel in races or games.

3. Discuss the concept of fairness. If you insist on making up the academic work that is missed because of behavior problems, the class will get the idea and "shape up."

4. Use a positive approach. If the whole class is doing the wrong thing except for one child, say: "I see that Janet knows what to do." Praise and building self-esteem is far more successful than recrimination.

5. Introduce the idea that adults also feel angry and "uptight." Capitalize on their desire to act grown-up by showing them how you and other adults cope with difficulties.

6. Find socially acceptable outlets for their emotions. A punching bag, set of drums, woodworking projects and other channels for self-expression can go a long way in displacing anger and aggression.

This above all; remember to maintain your sense of humor. Try to think of one funny thing that happened during the day as you drive home. In reflecting on the day's events look for something ludicrous or outrageous. This will give you a sense of balance. And, remember, tomorrow is a new day and there are sure to be difficult challenges and different tensions, but there will also be different things to laugh at.

how to prevent group unrest

Pupils basically want five things. If you deny most of them, you will have the class united against you. They basically want: (1) to be heard; (2) to have a "piece of the action"; (3) to be free to choose; (4) to have an opportunity to "do their thing"; and (5) to be accepted, if not loved.

Use these guidelines as insurance that you are meeting these needs of today's pupil.

1. Pupils want to be heard. A frequent complaint heard is, "I don't know one teacher in this school who has time to listen to me." Other students complain of classroom practices that tend to "put down" the child, allow no time for individual attention, and frighten or silence the students by use of set, one-way preconceived answers. Unfortunately, some adults fear that their positions of authority may be usurped and they close their minds to what young people may be trying to tell them.

2. They want to have "a piece of the action." Students feel they want to be involved. In San Mateo High School, California, they tutor elementary school pupils, work as teacher aides, and assist in athletics. In Wilson High School, Portland, Oregon, short-term mini-courses on subject matter not usually available in the regular curriculum are taught by students with special competencies in these areas.

3. Students want to be free to choose. When one of your objectives is to recognize and satisfy the need for making choices, the list of educational opportunities is endless. Choices that pupils could make might include books to read, questions to ask, experiments to do, community resources to explore, audio-visual equipment to use, projects to undertake, study contracts to sign, research to pursue, skills to practice, schedules to follow, papers to write, poems to compose, pictures to paint, and exercises to do.

4. They want to have an opportunity to do their own thing. Children want to be themselves. We must help them. Do some high schools still refuse to put mirrors into restrooms for fear the students will linger too long over their hair? Headstart teachers install a full-length mirror in their classrooms in order that disadvantaged children may have a good look at themselves and begin to develop a positive self-image. In too many classrooms the student's self-image is not only ignored, it is demeaned. Don't put out your pupil's "light." Respect it even if it is different from yours.

5. They want to be accepted, if not loved. Children want to be cared about. Studies indicate that youngsters who come from lower-income homes receive less physical attention, less eye-to-eye contact, less verbal attention from their teachers than do youngsters from advantaged homes. You have noticed, we are sure, that, while pupils desire positive recognition and acclaim, they will try for negative recognition rather than be ignored. A few years ago, a high school senior in Boston was expelled from the cafeteria because he was caught, for the third time, throwing food. The teacher on duty wrote, "Johnny is belligerent and impossible." Further conversations with the guidance counselor revealed: "John's brother was a big football hero. John felt he was a 'nuthin.' He was gaining attention by breaking the rules."

If you remember to respect the dignity and worth of your pupils no matter how repulsive some of their actions are, you will not have to worry about their staging a mutiny. Unless, of course, you are in charge of the lunchroom. This thankless, difficult task is fraught with danger and frustration in virtually every school. The following section should be helpful.

how to ease tensions in the lunchroom

Make things easy for yourself and the children by solving these three simple problems:

Where to sit.   (Assign regular seats, or at least the same table every day.)

How to line up to get food at the counters. (Talk this over with the dietician and do it the same way every day.)

How and where to empty trays after eating. (Be sure there are enough garbage cans.)

You are now ready to establish ground rules regarding running, shouting, fighting, and throwing food. Introduce background music while the pupils are eating.

Ask the pupils to bring in some of their favorite records. While quiet background music is fine while they are eating, you will need something a little more lively after they have emptied their trays. They may bring in disco or rock records. Have the lunchroom aides select two or three children from each class to dance for their school-mates in the central open area. Later on you can allow individual classes to dance.

After a while, encourage children to come to the microphone to sing or to tell riddles or jokes. The audience can sing as a spontaneous chorus to the music or in accompaniment to the soloist. Some classes may dance only after they finish eating and cleaning up.

Once a week have a mystery guest appear in a paper-bag mask. The children attempt to identify the masked guest who may be a pupil, parent, teacher, or other dignitary.

No matter what you try, there will always be a few children who must eat in isolation for a week or two. Some children just can't sit in so crowded an atmosphere without doing something foolish. Set up a private area for these few children to eat in.

Each lunchroom situation is unique. You may not be able to use these suggestions exactly as they appear here. Do try to get the flavor of what we are suggesting.

Group disciplinary problems are no more than a cluster of individuals with problems. Try to see it that way and keep your sense of humor.

4

making yourself
perfectly clear

"If only the children in my class understood what I meant!"
"They always take things the wrong way." "I wish they would listen
to me more carefully." These are statements that we have heard
teachers make over and over. While much of the blame falls on the
pupils' lack of attentiveness, there are steps you can take that will
make your messages loud and clear and unmistakable. These are
easy-to-apply steps that you can begin using today!

keys to giving directions that are followed

The most important aspect of teaching is the giving of clear
directions which will not lead to confusion and misunderstanding.
Good directions can save the teacher much time and effort in
repeating herself and clarifying what is meant. Follow these steps to
clarity.

1. Make certain that YOU understand what it is you expect
from the pupils. Read the workbook directions first to yourself, for
example.

2. Don't begin to speak until everyone is listening. Having
pupils clear their desks before you begin explanations helps to remove
distracting elements.

3. Speak clearly and loudly enough for everyone to hear you. Move your lips so that even the pupils with undiagnosed, partial hearing losses (about 15 percent of the school population) can understand you.

4. Use understandable language that is familiar to your pupils. Carefully explain any unknown terms. Write page numbers on the board so that the more forgetful pupils can refer to them after you have completed your directions.

5. Tell the pupils the object of the lesson. Show them the finished product they are trying to produce. Write the aim of the lesson on the board. Demonstrate the technique for them.

6. Don't try to cover too much with one set of directions. If the project is complex, break the job up into parts. Try duplicating directions so that each pupil will have an outline or guide to follow at his seat.

7. Have the pupils repeat the directions. Ask them questions to see if they understand, e.g., "What happens next?" What must you look out for?"

8. Invite pupils to ask you questions. Train them to ask questions BEFORE they begin to work.

9. For bigger projects, set up a bulletin board or chart with the directions laid out for reference.

10. Give additional practice by directing other tasks in a similar manner. We use the skill of following directions so much in life situations that teaching it again and again is warranted.

ways to express anger without sarcasm

Instead of trying to suppress anger altogether, teachers can express it in nondestructive ways. The use of sarcasm is destructive and must be avoided. This expression should bring some relief to the teacher, some insight to the pupil and no harmful aftereffects to either.

In expressing anger, we consciously need to avoid provoking waves of resentment and revenge. We want to get our point across, and then let the storm subside.

In times of stress, avoid "teacher burnout" by acknowledging these basic truths:

1. Accept the fact that in the natural course of events, pupils will, on occasion, make us uncomfortable, annoyed, irritated, angry, and even furious.
2. You are entitled to these feelings without guilt, shame, or regret. They are normal, natural feelings.
3. You are entitled to express your feelings, with one caveat. No matter how angry you get, do NOT insult the pupil's personality or character. To use sarcasm would do so.

There are some very specific, wholesome ways to deal with your anger. The first step in any annoying situation is to describe clearly how it affects you. Add nothing else. When George started tapping his pencil on his desk, his teacher said, "The noise makes me very uncomfortable." George gave one more tap and stopped. This method was effective because his teacher didn't tell George what to do. She described her discomfort and took it for granted that he would respond. Compare this approach to a more prevalent one:

"What's the matter with you? Don't you have anything better to do? Can't you sit still? Are you three years old? Stop it this minute."

Our friend George demonstrated to himself that he stopped of his own volition, not because of orders. Instead of belittling the pupil, the teacher used these four simple rules:

> Describe what you see.
> Describe what you feel.
> Describe what needs to be done.
> Do not attack the person.

Expressing anger without sarcasm or insult is not easy; it goes against natural inclinations and what we frequently observe. You must learn a new language that will enable you to give vent to your anger without damaging your dignity. Teachers who have mastered the new language have gained greater control over themselves. They feel capable of expressing their anger effectively and helpfully.

We heard a junior high school teacher tell of this incident. "Ronald likes to 'put me on.' He knows I don't like foul language. After one such remark I said, 'That kind of talk makes me uncomfortable.' The next time he started to say something in that vein, he stopped and said, 'I forgot, Mrs. Keyes doesn't like that.' "

With a little practice you will be able to integrate this kind of response into your repertoire.

how to back up your instructions

Every teacher needs to know how to back up her words when pupils choose not to respond to verbal limit-setting. You must spell out the consequences. For example,

> Teacher: *Andy, keep your hands to yourself. If you poke your neighbor you will have to sit by yourself. It's up to you.*
>
> Andy: *Okay, Miss Kent. (However, he pokes Fred and Carl two minutes later.)*
>
> Teacher: *Andy, you annoyed Fred and Carl. You have chosen to sit by yourself in the back of the room.*

When you provide a pupil with a choice, you place the responsibility where it belongs—on the pupil. It is your responsibility, however, to inform him of the consequences.

Pick out a consequence that you are comfortable with. Select one that the child does not like but that is not physically or psychologically harmful. Offer it in a matter-of-fact, calm voice. Put it into effect as soon as possible after the child chooses to disregard your instructions. Try these kinds of consequences:

Isolation ward	– The pupil must sit in a remote corner of the room for 10 to 20 minutes.
Loss of privilege	– Free time, recess, field trip, etc. Make sure it's something the child is sorry to miss.
Stay after school	– This is especially good for kids who do not do their work in class. You must be willing to stay until the work is finished.

Home consequences – Call or send a note home. Arrange with parents to provide a follow-up: no TV, stay in bedroom, loss of privileges.

why brief commands are best

When you give instructions to your class, don't overwhelm them with a lot of words. If you do, they are likely to remember the last few words only.

Pupils are assaulted with all kinds of sounds. They carry large radios and play them loud. They listen to and dance to disco music that is deafening. Their parents are frequently telling them what to do. By the time they get to school they are in no mood to hear the teacher's long-winded commands. They merely turn you off as if they had mechanical hearing aids.

You can counter this by saying less with greater emphasis. When you do speak, be sure that all the pupils are listening if you wish to address the whole class. Many teachers find that flicking the light switch, ringing a bell, or playing a chord on the piano are more effective techniques for getting attention than speaking. Above all, don't yell.

If you read this number aloud to your class—186,542,947—they would be most likely to remember the 947 part of the number. This, of course, is the least important part. The 186 million is the more significant part of the whole number. The same is true when you give commands to your class. Keep them short and put the important words at the beginning or end of the command, not in the middle. Be sure to use strong positive action words, such as, "You WILL go to your seat." Note that "you" and "where to go" are given emphasis by being placed as the first and last words.

You don't need two paragraphs to say: "Class, stand." An extremely complex operation can be put in gear with a simple command. General Eisenhower launched the invasion of Europe with a simple 23-word sentence:

"You will enter the continent of Europe and undertake operations aimed at the heart of Germany and the destruction of her armed forces." That 23-word order launched more than 4 million troops. Surely you can send 30 pupils into action with just as few words.

how to set rules that are kept

It's one thing to issue commands but it is another to make sure they are completed.

Rules must deal with specifics. They cannot be vague, general, or abstruse. In a classroom they are likely to be: follow directions, sit in seat, take turns, keep hands to yourself. Other rules you might have might be: complete assignments, don't leave the room without permission, work independently. As the teacher you must know how to respond when pupils are disruptive and don't follow your carefully executed rules.

There are four general methods

Hints – "Everyone should be working."

Questions – "Would you please get to work?"

I messages – "I want you to get your pencil out and begin writing."

Demands – "Get to work, now!"

The first three are best because most children will respond to them. Demands imply consequences for noncompliance, and all too often a teacher is not prepared to follow through. Assertive discipline has only one commandment: "Thou shalt not make a demand thou are not ready to follow up on."

How you enunciate the rules is as important as *what* you say. Put conviction in your voice. Don't sound as if you are pleading or whining. Don't put a question in your voice. Sound as if you mean what you are saying.

Try the broken record technique. Keep repeating what you want the pupils to do, using the same words and inflection. Don't let yourself get sidetracked by the pupil's response. He or she might question, plead, negate, or feign surprise, but you stick to your guns and merely repeat the rule or direction just like a broken record. With this technique, preface your statement with, "That's not the point . . ." or "I see, but . . ." "You're right, but . . ." Enhance the broken record technique with direct eye contact. If you don't know the eye color of each of the difficult pupils in your class then you haven't been using a valuable tool—direct eye contact. If necessary, add a gesture, use the pupil's name, or, as a last resort, place your face close to his and repeat yourself for the last time.

Use positive verbal assertions. What do you do when pupils *do* follow your rules? Unfortunately, most teachers do nothing to foster the continuation of the good behavior they want and need from their pupils. By responding positively to positive rule-following you are giving your kids the attention they want and need. Select a response you are comfortable with and plan how you will use it. Make sure it is something the pupil wants and give it as soon as possible after the rule is followed. Do it every time.

ways to use praise effectively

Praise can backfire. Tell a pupil he is "good" and he denies it. Praise a teenager for his science project and he is quick to point out its defects. Some praise actually brings about ill feeling. Some praise can bring about feelings of anxiety. Why? Because it tends to evaluate. For example: "You are always so sweet." "You are such a good boy." Such evaluation is uncomfortable. The evaluator sits in judgment. To be judged is to be anxious. It puts the pupil under an obligation to live up to the impossible. No one can always be sweet or good.

To use praise effectively you should *describe* and not evaluate. Deal with events instead of personality. Describe feelings, don't evaluate character. Give a realistic picture of the accomplishment; don't glorify the person. Let's contrast the two types of praise.

	Effective	**Ineffective**
Teacher:	"Thank you for washing the chalk board. It looks great."	"You are a marvelous monitor."
Pupil: (silently)	(I did a good job. I can do some things well.)	(I'm not always marvelous. My teacher isn't so smart.)

	Effective	Ineffective
Teacher:	"Your humorous essay was very funny. It made me laugh out loud."	"You are a born writer."
Pupil:	(I can make people laugh, sometimes.)	(Last year's teacher didn't think so.)
Teacher:	"I appreciate your stacking the library books. We were running late and there were so many books."	"You are a terrific kid."
Pupil:	(I can be helpful. She appreciates what I did today.)	(I can't be terrific all of the time.)

Do you see how descriptive praise is likely to lead to a realistic self-image? The remarks in parentheses show how the youngster is likely to react to the stated praise. Praise has two parts: our words and the pupil's conclusions. In a real sense, praise is what the pupil says to himself after we have spoken. Our words should describe clearly what we like and appreciate about his work, efforts, achievement, considerations, or creation. We describe the specific event and our specific feelings. He draws conclusions about his personality and character. Dr. Haim Ginott made some of these findings popular in the 1960's. Good teachers have been using them ever since.

The more disruptive or deviant the child, the more likely he is to reject praise of any kind. It is ironic that the children who are least responsive to adult praise are those whose behavior needs modification.

The best way to reach these children is to pair praise with a delivery of rewards. This could be a simple point system. Teacher praise should be presented immediately prior to the delivery of the reward. The pupil's appropriate behavior that is being reinforced should be described in specific terms. The teacher should clearly communicate approval of it, and the point delivery should follow immediately. Never give a point first followed by praise. For example, "Joey, you worked hard on your spelling assignment. You got 14 out of 15 words correct. You are doing good work. That's three points for accuracy, and a bonus point for doing better than yesterday. Keep up the good work!"

After a while, pair praise and points every time points are awarded. This pairing should simply become an automatic part of the point-awarding process. As the frequency of giving points is gradually reduced (if this is your goal), occasional unpaired praises should be given between the times praise and points are awarded. This will help maintain the child's appropriate behavior between the delivery of points. It will also help the child adapt to the fading procedure.

The systematic use of powerful, effective teacher praise is probably the most important and significant single thing the teacher can do to build in the long term maintenance of changed child behavior.

Here are some sample praise statements that follow the thinking we have described in this chapter.

Marie, your math paper was 100 percent correct.

That's good thinking, Jerry.

I appreciate the way you sit quietly and listen while I'm giving a lesson.

It makes me very happy to see you working so well.

Alan walked to his seat very quietly. Thank you, Alan.

Frank knows how to follow instructions.

That was a courteous thing to do for Anne, Mark.

All of Row Two is sitting with their materials ready.

how to apply rules correctly

There are certain guidelines that should be followed in setting and following up on rules for your pupils. For example, rules should be clearly defined and stated in behavioral terms. Vague rules relating to ambiguously defined behavior are probably no more effective than a complete absence of rules. Examples of both clearly-defined, behavior-specific rules and vague, general rules are presented below:

Good Rules	Poor Rules
Listen carefully to teacher instructions.	Behave in class.
Raise your hand before asking a question.	Be considerate of others.
Pay attention to assignments.	Do what you are told.
Do not talk to others during work time.	Don't disturb others.
Finish your "do now" work.	Work hard.

A good rule identifies a specific behavior or activity in a very precise way. Remember that the correct interpretation of a rule's meaning should require as little inference on the part of the pupil as possible. It should be perfectly clear!

It's a good idea to involve the class in the process of developing rules for both classroom and nonclassroom areas. Children are more committed to the rules if they participate in their development.

Train your pupils to follow rules that are directed at them in a nonverbal way. For example, write "SSS" on the chalkboard. Teach them that the three S's mean: stand, stretch, sit. A big "D" on the board tells the class they may have drinks of water if they go quietly in turn to the fountain. "C.U." is the signal for cleaning up after an art period. It's surprising how quickly these signals pass around the room although the teacher has said nothing. You can develop the signals you need for your own classroom.

By applying your rules fairly you will find that your class has greater respect for you and for each other.

5

approaching homework as a factor of discipline

The assignment of homework has many uses. It should be used to extend the classroom learning, to reinforce what was learned in class, to provide enrichment or remediation, but NOT as a punishment for misbehavior. It is a mistake to use additional homework as punishment. Such a practice only reinforces the negative feelings that some pupils have for school. Remember, problem pupils already possess enough negative attitudes. Therefore, if you are going to punish, use a form of punishment that is not a part of the classroom learning experience. In this way you may solve a problem rather than compound one.

how maintaining standards for homework strengthens classroom discipline

You have done just part of the job if you assign homework and then check to see that it is done and corrected. Your pupils should learn on the very first day of school what your precise standards for homework are. Discuss your standards, explain the reason for them, write them on the board, and have pupils read them back to you. Your standards might include whether it is done in pencil or pen, the use of a ruler, the kind of paper, the type of notebook, the required heading, allowances for erasing, procedures for having parents sign the homework page, etc. This is a far cry from accepting any scrap of paper with some writing on it. Sadly, many of our colleagues around the country have fallen into the trap of accepting just about anything as valid homework.

If a youngster goes home and feels that he can turn in any scribbled sheet "just as long as it contains the correct answers" he is reinforcing poor classroom discipline. He is also learning poor work habits that will remain with him in adulthood.

Before you give the first homework assignment of the year make sure that every pupil knows exactly what is expected of him. Your standards should be so clear that even the slowest pupil will know what is required. It is generally useful to pass around some samples of last year's homework. By looking at the actual paper that another child handed in, your class will have a visual picture of what their homework should look like. Because it was done by one of their peers they can identify with it and try to emulate the sample shown.

Demanding certain standards for homework will improve your classroom control. When the youngsters realize that yours is not a classroom where "anything goes," they will behave better. You are reinforcing this concept when you demand high standards for homework. Here, too, the pupils see that they can't get away with just "any old thing" and call it homework. In a sense, you are giving two kinds of homework. One reinforces the math, language arts or other curriculum area. The second, by your insisting on certain standards of excellence, reinforces your standards of discipline. As the child practices care in doing his homework, he is also practicing how to behave in your classroom.

In addition to the quality of homework handed in, you should also be concerned with consistency. Pupils do not like changes. They are really creatures of habit. Try to assign homework regularly in modest amounts. This is far better than giving massive assignments occasionally and no homework the rest of the time. If you are in an intermediate school you may be the only teacher who gives homework every week night. Take this as a compliment. Your pupils will notice every week night that you are the one teacher who means business. Weekends and holidays should be homework free.

The format of the homework is something that you will want to work out for yourself. Some teachers insist on homework books where the pages are sewn in. Others like the ease of collecting loose-leaf pages rather than awkward notebooks. In any case, you should occasionally insist on collecting the homework. After checking it, tell the pupils to place the corrected homework in their homework folders. These folders can be as simple as a large sheet of construction paper that is folded in half. Or, they might be actual manila file folders. You can also use large manila envelopes. The homework folder should have the child's name on it.

Keeping samples of each pupil's homework in a separate folder serves many purposes. For one thing, a survey of the youngster's homework papers for the marking period or quarter should show some growth or improvement. On Open School Night such a folder is invaluable. Parents are frequently amazed at what their children's homework looks like by the time it gets to school. Also, a circumspect teacher can reach into a classmate's folder to show the parent how careful other classmates are. There is also a psychological benefit when the pupil knows that his homework is being kept in a folder. As the folder grows, the pupil develops more respect for his homework, his classwork, and, most important, for himself.

ways to encourage pupils to do their homework and grow in self-respect

As an experienced teacher you have no doubt used a variety of techniques to get your pupils to do their homework. For many teachers this takes the form of marking kids down for not bringing in their assignments, giving them a zero or demerit, or so on. We have compiled a list here of positive steps other teachers have used to motivate their pupils to do their homework assignments.

1. Relate the assignment to the day's lesson after you are sure that the pupils understand what was taught.
2. Word the assignment in the form of a puzzle or brain teaser to stimulate pupil involvement.
3. Use extrinsie rewards for improvement, such as star charts or a point system.
4. Motivate by your example. Point out that you do homework too. Indicate your need for lesson plans.
5. Use the youngster's current interests to teach particular skills. Assign math work in the form of batting averages or recipes.

6. Assume a positive attitude. Write lavish comments on the homework papers like: "Great Improvement" or "Excellent Work." Send "happy notes" home praising the work done by the pupil.

7. Make the checking of homework a regular part of the school day. If pupils feel that the work will not be checked, they are less likely to do it.

Dominic was a fifth grader who did as he pleased at school and at home. His divorced mother was so tired when she came home from work that a "session" with Dominic over homework was the last thing on her mind. Consequently, Dominic was frequently unprepared when he got to school. Because homework was checked early in the day, his day usually started with a scolding from the teacher. Things usually went downhill from there. After a few weeks of this vicious cycle his teacher tried a new approach. She made the four or five pupils who "forgot" assignments "homework helpers." Their job was to help collect the homework papers of their classmates and check the papers for completeness and accuracy. The teacher explained that the homework helpers would have their papers checked by the teacher first for thoroughness and accuracy. Dominic and the other homework helpers loved the idea and never came unprepared again.

By establishing strict control over the handing in of homework you will also help your pupils grow in self-control. This self-control will begin the night before when the pupils do their assignments away from your presence. If they can be made to do this regularly they will begin to control their other impulses while in class and under your direct supervision.

why you must check homework daily if you want to maintain classroom order

During those strategic first few days, list clearly a few handy rules to cover situations that can really mushroom later. A caution: You will immediately put yourself on the defensive by mentioning homework. The pupils are well aware of the inevitability of homework and expect you to deal with breaches of homework rules. If you allow any skipping of homework to go unnoticed you are lost.

One satisfactory system is to assign a half-hour detention after school in your classroom. After a while, pupils begin to realize that it is easier to do the homework in the comfort of their own home than it is to sit in your classroom for the same thirty minutes.

If more than one day goes by and you haven't checked the homework, your pupils will lose their motivation to do your assignments. That is why you should check homework each day. If the pupils see that you don't really mean what you say about homework they will carry this over to other areas as well. Good classroom order depends upon pupils believing what their teacher says.

Here's a simple way to check homework of the class as a whole. It does not take the place of physically going over each pupil's homework paper. We call it, "Do Now." Review the homework of the night before and extract two examples (if math) or two comprehension questions. Write these on the board and have pupils answer them as soon as they come into the room. This helps set the tone for the period or day.

Pupils should be in their assigned seats when the bell rings, with all required materials on their desks: pen, paper, book, folder, or notebook. If this rule isn't enforced, you'll never be able to begin the class period effectively. While you are struggling to herd pupils into seats, get them to haul out their books, and quiet them down, others in the class will become restless and begin talking. You have thus lost your power as the dominating force. It's far more effective to swing the door shut dramatically as the bell is ringing, and have something to say to the class as a whole during the expectant lull. Don't let pupils fall into the habit of clustering around your desk or confronting you with personal problems until you have had a chance to get the class underway. Make an announcement, conduct a quick review, GO OVER THE HOMEWORK, anything to make you the leader—then let the class get to work on their "Do Now" board assignment.

While they are doing the "Do Now," you can issue out-of-class passes, talk to someone, return papers, or quickly review notes for a discussion or short lecture. It's better to begin the class promptly and finish a little early. During the last ten minutes in a relaxed atmosphere at the end of the period or day, pupils are usually more quiet and orderly than when they first come in. Train them to use that time to think about the homework that is due tomorrow.

Sometimes, in spite of all your efforts, a pupil will just not do his or her homework. It is a good idea to involve the parents of such pupils. In order to cut down on letter-writing we are including three letters here that you can duplicate for future use.

HOMEWORK NOTICE

_____
Date

Dear _____ ,

    This is to inform you that, in spite of my efforts, your son/daughter _____ of Class ____ has not submitted complete homework assignments in _____ on the following dates: _____ .
subject

    Since our school views homework as a very important part of our program of studies, as well as a factor in determining the grade received in the subject, we urge your assistance in correcting this situation.

                Sincerely,

                (Mrs.) Carol Grossman
                Teacher

– – – – – – Please detach and return to school – – – – – – –

Pupil's Name _____ Class ____
I have read the homework notice dated: _____

_____
Parent's Signature

Figure 5-1

Note how this letter, while a printed form letter, allows for personal contact and follow-up in the last paragraph. Another plus we found in this letter is that it takes into account the student who does well academically but does not behave well. The second paragraph refers to the denial of Honors Awards to such pupils.

NOTICE OF POSSIBLE FAILING CONDUCT MARK

_____
Date

Dear _____ :

I regret to inform you that your child, _____ of Class _____, will receive a conduct mark that is less than satisfactory for the current marking period unless there is sufficient improvement in class behavior.

Since the pupil's own progress as well as the rights of others to an uninterrupted education are affected by repeated misconduct, it is the policy of the school to deny all Honors Awards to pupils who receive a conduct mark of less than satisfactory. Furthermore, promotion at the end of the school year may be denied for serious, uncorrected misconduct.

I shall be happy to confer with you in person or by telephone during school hours so that we may plan together for your child's improvement. If you wish such a conference, please advise me by return mail, or by calling the school at 442-8481.

Sincerely,

Andrew Walker
Teacher

Figure 5-2

NOTICE OF POSSIBLE SUBJECT FAILING GRADE

_____
Date

Dear _____ ,

This is to inform you that your child, _____
of Class _____ , may receive a failing grade in _____
for the current market period unless there is satisfactory improvement in the area(s) of student performance noted as
follows:

_____ Preparation for classwork
_____ Participation in classwork
_____ Fulfillment of assignments
_____ Test Marks

_____ _____

I shall be happy to confer with you in person or by
telephone during school hours so that we may plan for your
child's success in his/her studies. If you wish such a conference, please so advise me by return mail or by calling the
school at 698-1234.

Sincerely,

Bernard Monahan
Teacher

Figure 5-3

A strong point in this letter is that it recognizes homework or
"preparation for classwork" as a major cause of possible failure. Also,
the last of the five areas is left blank so that the teacher can add one of
his own or elaborate on one of the areas checked.

what to do about late assignments

Mary Cooke always handed in her homework assignments. They
were neat and complete. The exasperating part of it was that they

were always late. Mary never handed a paper in on time. Her teacher good-naturedly referred to her as the "late Mary Cooke." Mary smiled at this and continued her practice of being a day or two late.

Her teacher felt strongly that the classroom is supposed to prepare you for life in the outside world. Being late all the time is hardly a trait that is valued in the business world. She instituted a new policy. "Homework that is late will be graded and ten points will be taken off for each day it is late." This stimulated many of the late pupils to hand their work in on time. It kept Mary on time occasionally but not always. Her teacher did not give up. She put into practice every one of these rules until she finally broke every child in her class of the late assignment habit.

1. Late papers must be signed by a parent.
2. A formal letter to the teacher must accompany every late assignment explaining the reason for lateness.
3. Offenders will be kept with their homeroom teacher for twenty minutes and therefore may be late for one of their favorite activities: gym, library, lunch, recess, etc.
4. Late assignments will be returned later than assignments handed in on time.
5. After school sessions will be held for the pupil and teacher to discuss possible reasons for the pupil's behavior.

using the homework book as a discipline tool

Wouldn't it be great if you had a telephone hour each morning as part of your teaching program? You could then chat with the parents of each of your pupils and thus insure excellent behavior and perfect conduct. Unfortunately, this type of direct communication doesn't seem to be feasible.

But every child in your room carries home each day an instrument of communication that you can tap—his homework notebook. Early in the term, establish a procedure where parents sign their child's homework. When you check the homework, write comments on the page. The parents will get into the habit of looking at the previous night's homework to read your comments. This is especially true in the elementary school.

Encourage dialogue with the parents by writing specific, individual comments. Ask short, simple questions. They will be glad to write back. Be sure to offer praise when you see some improvement in conduct. If the parents sense that you don't recognize their efforts they will get discouraged and you will have missed an opportunity for valuable help.

Write your comments neatly and in blue ink. Too many teachers insist on writing to parents in red pencil, blue crayon, red ink, or some other medium that has the same effect as a loud, coarse shout. A neat, normal-sized handwriting has the effect of a well-modulated voice. Parents, like all of us, want to feel rewarded for the effort they expend. If you see any improvement be sure to mention it.

Naturally, you will have to check to see that every child takes his notebook home every day, otherwise your lines of communication will be down. Some pupils like to look for a secret place in the classroom where they can hide their notebook until the next morning. But as an alert, experienced teacher, you will preclude any such tampering with your "discipline tools."

how a missed homework assignment can lead to self-improvement

Miss Hansen took it personally when an important homework assignment was not done on time. Through the years she noted that pupils never gave as much thought to the missed assignment as she did. Last year, Miss Hansen developed an Assignment Analysis Sheet that has been a surefire success. She hands the sheet out to all pupils who miss an assignment. She now has zero repeaters. That is, when a youngster gets an Assignment Analysis Sheet to fill out, he never misses another assignment. Now, you know from your own experience that it's usually the same handful of pupils who "forget" to do their homework. We asked Miss Hansen for permission to reprint her sheet for your use. It consists of six simple questions. The youngsters must answer each question in one or more complete sentences.

After using this form for a while, some teachers report that pupils find filling it out more taxing than doing the actual assignment. When asked about this, the pupils revealed that this form makes them think about themselves, whereas the homework does not make them "look inside."

This is certainly a worthwhile objective—getting pupils to look inside or analyze their motives. Frequently, when a youngster pauses

---

Assignment Analysis Sheet

1. Was there anything you did not understand about this assignment?

2. Did you have trouble getting the necessary books or materials?

3. How could this assignment be changed to make it more interesting?

4. What did you do instead of doing this assignment?

5. What must you do to change your attitude about schoolwork?

6. When will you be able to make this assignment up?

Figure 5-4

long enough to analyze why he is doing something, or in this case, not doing something, his attitude changes. Miss Hansen tells her class that if a second occasion should arise where the Sheet is necessary, she will insist that it be signed by a parent. So far, no youngster in her class has missed a second assignment. She also insists that the Sheet be filled out completely, neatly, and with no erasures or crossing out. Some youngsters have to redo the Sheet until she finds it acceptable. Her standards are high!

ways to improve the quality of homework

Did you ever pause to look at the kinds of homework assignments you give? Generally, they fall into two categories: the necessary but dull, and the imaginative and long-range kinds of assigments. Surely if you're assigning math homework it is hard to be very creative. Most math assignments take the form of "Page 132, Problems 10 through 15." In subjects like language arts, science, and social studies, there are projects and other long-range assignments that tap your youngsters' creativity and stimulate their interest.

It's not so much the quantity of homework that turns pupils off, as much as it is the quality of the thinking required of them to complete it. We all like puzzles and games. We don't think of the Sunday crossword puzzles as a homework assignment. Yet, many of us do it with regularity as if it were assigned work.

A junior high school math teacher describes some innovations she made in the area of homework:

"My pre-algebra pupils had always seen mathematics as strictly a problem-solving subject. I felt that, regardless of whether the pupils would be going on in math or not, it would be of value for them to see the subject as a part of the development of civilization—to learn something about the background of mathematics and its different branches. So, this last quarter of the year I have assigned reports for pupils to do in pairs, groups, or as individuals. I have given them about six weeks to do research for these reports, allowing some class library time, after showing various math books and magazines to them in class. Their topics range from the general history of mathematics, to form or number systems other than ten, to mathematics in nature. They are using the overhead projector, filmstrips, dittoes, and posters for presenting their topics. These reports and projects have probably generated more involvement than any other procedure I've used. The whole subject of math is beginning to make sense to these kids for the first time. They are actually competitive in completing their projects."

Another way of having pupils take greater pride in the appearance of their homework is to post samples of their homework around the room. It's amazing how many pupils get a lift from seeing their work on display. When they know what your standards are for displayed homework they will aim to meet them.

Still another way to improve the quality of homework is to give the pupils a role in the assignment of work. We've seen this done with a small committee of pupils who meet with the teacher each morning to devise that night's homework. The committee membership changes monthly so that every child gets a chance to serve. You'll be surprised at how attitudes toward homework change once a pupil has served on the committee.

The whole area of homework is one that has sparked controversy since the days of the one-room schoolhouse. Parents and parent groups vacillate between criticizing teachers who give too much homework and those who don't give enough. Principals usually insist on the assignment of homework but hesitate to state what constitutes "enough." Pupils groan and complain about the length of the assignment as it is given and then go home and dash it off in ten minutes. Other pupils take pride in their homework or else dawdle for an hour over the simplest review of the day's work in class.

To sum up, there are just a few basic commandments about homework that teachers occasionally forget to follow. These are:

1. Be consistent in your assignments. Don't pile it on one night and then go a week without giving any homework.

2. Make sure your pupils know ahead of time just what you expect of them in the area of homework. Go over form and method before assigning any.

3. Be sure to check homework daily. Check to see if it was done and if it was done correctly. You may use monitors to assist you.

4. Don't use homework as a punishment. This merely increases hostility and is self-defeating.

5. Everyone loves a break in routines. Once in a while announce that there is no homework tonight. Give some reason and watch the smiles break out. For this to be effective it can't be overdone.

6. Involve parents in the homework. Have them sign papers that are not acceptable.

6

preventing problems vs. punishing pupils

Teacher: *Kevin, what are you doing?*

Kevin: *I'm going to the pencil sharpener.*

Teacher: *You know the class rule. You're supposed to sharpen all the pencils you need before we begin work.*

Kevin: *I only have two pencils. I broke them during math.*

Teacher: *All Right! Hurry up and get back to your seat.* Kevin continues walking towards the sharpener. As the teacher turns to answer a pupil's question, Kevin begins a conversation with two pupils near the window. The teacher notices and turns red with anger.

Teacher: *Kevin, I told you to sharpen your pencils and get back in your seat. I mean it.*

Kevin: *O.K. O.K., I'm goin'.*

Does this little exchange sound familiar? Too often it is typical of a classroom scene in which the child who is acting out is the star and gets the last word as well as the admiration of much of the audience. Kids like Kevin tend to take up too much of your valuable time; time that could be spent working with other children. You are pulled into endless confrontations with such pupils in vain attempts to control their behavior.

how to anticipate trouble before it starts

The teacher had the right idea when she referred to a class rule about sharpening pencils before starting to work. But this was not enough. A more basic rule was violated or, perhaps it doesn't exist in her classroom; that is, "Pupils may not leave their seats without permission."

If she had set up such a rule and stopped Kevin before he marched down the aisle, much of the rancor could have been avoided. More and more, we have heard from master teachers that the best advice is to prevent trouble before it starts. You, as the adult, must anticipate what could possibly go wrong, and then prevent that first misstep from taking place. In this case, if Kevin had raised his hand, the teacher could then have allowed or not allowed him to go to the sharpener. In either case, she would have been in charge. She would have been the star and not Kevin, for she would have had the best lines—the class would have heard the teacher get the last word. If necessary, she could have casually escorted him to the sharpener in order to better supervise his movements.

Another good way of anticipating trouble before it starts is to closely observe your pupils as they enter the room in the morning or at the beginning of the period. With just a little practice you will be able to tell when Ronald is having a good or a bad day. While you can't give in completely to the whims and moods of your pupils, you can modify your demands and expectations for a particular day.

Try to develop a good ear for pupils' conversations. It is a form of eavesdropping, but it is also in the best interest of the class. By listening in you will learn a great deal about pupil interactions on a daily basis. You will become aware of which children the pupils respect and look up to as the leaders of the class. Even the worst-behaved pupils in your school look up to certain fellow pupils as the "bosses" of the schoolyard or playground or neighborhood center. You have to make sure that you are the only "boss" in the classroom. However, by capitalizing on the leadership potential of the nonacademic leaders you will see a positive carryover in your classroom.

Pupils never seem to run out of ways to grab the teacher's or class's attention in a negative way. It is important for the teacher to learn how to deal with such attention-getting behavior.

ways to extinguish attention-getting devices

Behavioral psychologists use a word we like: extinction. Defined in their terms, *the process of withholding rewards from previously rewarded behavior is referred to as placing the behavior in extinction.*

You can make some of your pupils' behavior as extinct as the American buffalo. Extinction can be used to reduce certain attention-getting behaviors that may be disruptive to your classroom. Extinction, in the form of ignoring, can be applied successfully to such irritating classroom behavior as dawdling, pencil tapping, asking irrelevant questions, and minor rule breaking. If the pupil does these things primarily to irritate the teacher and to get attention, then systematically ignoring them may be quite effective in reducing their frequency. You would not want to ignore some action that was disruptive to the whole class. Your judgment must prevail.

We can't tell you in advance how long it will take for a particular pupil to stop a given behavior. Be prepared to stick with extinction for a while until it has proven successful. Of course, certain "high magnitude" behaviors such as fighting, tantrums, and open defiance cannot be handled through extinction. As a general rule, extinction should be used when the behavior is minimally disruptive to the classroom atmosphere and is directed at getting your attention.

six things your disruptive pupils need

Why are those kids in your room so disruptive? Why are they so cool and cocky while we simmer and steam? What we do not always see is the fear that completely controls these acting-out, aggressive pupils. Underneath that cool exterior is usually a frightened little kid. Yes, these troublemakers who pose a real threat to our authority in the classroom are really afraid. Most of all they are afraid of themselves. In planning for and handling such a class or child we must recognize these six needs:

1. They need to feel that someone is in charge. They must have the structure that is missing elsewhere in their lives. They don't want to be closely watched or dominated but they do want to sense that someone nearby is responsible for them and their actions.

2. They need to feel that this "someone" will set and maintain limits for them. They fear their own sense of power and destructiveness. They really want some strong and fair person to keep them from harming themselves.

3. They must be shown how to separate the emotion they feel from the action they use to express the emotion. Someone must help them identify the emotion they are feeling and show approval or acceptance of the emotion while rejecting the action. For example, "It's O.K. for you to feel angry when John tore your paper. But kicking him in the stomach was the wrong thing to do."

4. They need to continually feel that someone is providing an appropriate role model. This helps them cope with frustration in a rational way. If they have a teacher who yells all the time and loses her temper very easily they feel that everyone is incapable of exercising self-control.

5. They need to be instructed repeatedly in how to deal with life's everyday frustrations. The teacher cannot assume that they will remember from one day to the next how to control their feelings. This will come much later.

6. They need to have their little successes in self-control recognized and rewarded. Even a simple word of sincere praise may be enough. This will provide some assurance that they are beginning to maintain control over their inner destructiveness.

Do these kids need punishment? Sometimes they do. The purpose of punishment has been twofold: to point out to the offender that a given behavior is unacceptable or wrong, and to inhibit him from repeating the behavior. A third more suitable and subtle purpose of punishment is to communicate to the pupil that the situation is not under his control. Often, this fact is one that the offender would like to have someone tell him.

If a pupil destroys a book he ought to pay for it. But instead of calling this punishment we would like the offender to realize in a more rational moment later on that he was wrong and that he should do something to make up for the damage. There is nothing wrong with pointing out to a pupil the amount of damage he has done, or insisting that he pay for it. What does matter is allowing the pupil to control his own actions and be able to give himself the credit for having made up for his wrongdoing. Forced apologies are harmful for the same reasons. Persuade him to make the apology if you wish, but be careful you don't reinforce the offense by spending too much time on this. Be certain he or she understands that you do not want him or her to apologize unless truly sorry.

Self-control is far better than control from an outside force or source.

how to create an atmosphere of self-control

As long as you teach children you can expect to be teaching self-control. You may not call it self-control but that will be the aim of your lesson. Expect to spend a block of time and energy on this facet with each and every class you have. Accept conduct-training, or any other name you give it, as a normal part of teaching. Placing such training in this perspective helps you overcome the feeling of imposition—that self-control training is an extra chore or waste of good instructional time. On the contrary, without such training, EVERYTHING else that you try to teach will be wasted.

In all groups there must be control. It can be imposed by others—outside control. This type of control comes from an authority figure. Or, an individual can impose control on himself—inside control (self-control). Point out to your pupils that the choice is theirs. The control can be personal, or by the authority of a teacher. Assure them that there WILL be control. Tell them that you will respect any decision they make as long as they live up to it. Pupils of all ages can accept these concepts if they are worded in language they understand. There are many classrooms where the pupils are ready for the responsibility of making this decision for themselves.

Self-control and a good learning atmosphere are synonymous. It is sometimes easier for you, the teacher, to exercise control over classroom situations. Some teachers are more comfortable in the role of disciplinarian. For them it is easier to exercise complete control at all times. Those teachers who succeed in having their pupils learn self-control enjoy their jobs more in the long run. They get more satisfaction by seeing their youngsters learn and develop habits of self-control. Every teacher we spoke to emphasized the wisdom of stressing expected conduct standards and procedures for the first several weeks of the term. They felt that the time spent in establishing basic control is rewarded many times over. The pupils learn far more and are happier doing so.

Your feelings of healthy self-respect are essential if you are to foster self-control in your pupils. Don't see every pupil's misdemeanor as an attack on your person or your psyche. You are not always the target. Clear your own thought of emotion before you handle a behavior incident.

forms of letters to parents that get action

At times, it is necessary to contact parents of problem children. Let's look at two letters that teachers have sent home.

Dear Mrs. Lopez:
Please come to school Monday morning at 9:00 A.M. I must talk to you about Julia's behavior. She has been impossible for the past two weeks. I don't know how I can keep her in this class anymore.
Sincerely,
M.T.W.

Figure 6-1

Dear Mrs. Lopez:
Please come to school so that we can talk about the work that Julia is doing. I am her science teacher. Monday morning at 9:00 A.M. would be a good time for me. I hope you can make it. If not, please call me at 442-6123 and we will make an appointment for a time that is better for you. If I don't get a call from you I will be expecting you at 9:00 A.M. on Monday in the Science Office.
I am looking forward to seeing you.
Sincerely,
T.F.S.

Figure 6-2

Which of the two letters would a parent feel less threatend to receive? The first one is abrupt and displays much of the teacher's insecurity. M.T.W. uses phrases like: "I must," "she has been impossible," and "I don't know how . . ."

These show her own frustration and anxiety. The tone of the letter resembles a summons to Traffic Court. It begins with a fixed appointment (not allowing for the parent's schedule) and ends with an empty threat (what will the teacher do with her if she doesn't keep her in the class?).

The second letter from T.F.S. can easily be mimeographed with just the dates, time, and name inserted and still be better received by the parent. The opening sentence gives the purpose of the letter in a positive, nonpunitive way. The second sentence identifies the writer. The next few lines offer a specific appointment with room for adjustment to suit the parent. The last sentence repeats the recommended time and pinpoints the precise location. The looking forward. . . is an amenity that costs nothing yet establishes the writer as a person and not a monster.

Of course, if you don't send out many of these letters each week it is certainly better to write out or type each letter individually. If you send out dozens of them, especially around the end of the marking period, you may want to duplicate them and fill in the specific details.

What can you do if, in spite of your efforts, you get no reply? Send a follow-up letter similar to this one.

Dear Mrs. Lopez:

On March 8, I sent you a letter asking you to come to school so that we could talk about Julia's work. I mailed one copy home and put one copy in Julia's notebook.

Because of my concern for Julia, and the possibility that she may get a failing mark on her report card, I am writing you this second letter. I have told the principal that I would not do anything until I spoke to you. The grades must go into the office in two weeks. Please call me 442-6123 as soon as you get this letter.

If you wish, write your preferred meeting time on the back of this note and return it with Julia tomorrow.

Sincerely,

T.F.S.

Figure 6-3

Notice that this second letter is a little more direct. The teacher doesn't mince any words about the need for the meeting. She makes it clear that on March 8th two copies of a letter went home, BUT she doesn't accuse the parent of ignoring the letter. She begins the second paragraph with her concern for the child's welfare yet makes it clear that inaction on the parent's part may result in a failing grade. The parent is made to feel responsible if she ignores this second notice. Instead of the teacher's setting an appointment that may not be kept, the mother is asked to pick the time. A time limit has been established when the teacher says the grades must be sent to the office in two weeks. The authority of the principal has been brought in subtly while the teacher remains "the good guy." It's always a good practice to clear letters that you send home with the principal *before* you do so. This is especially so if you use his or her name or office in the body of the letter.

Keep a copy of every letter that you send home. Also, put the date and method of transmittal on the back of the letter.

If a parent writes back a note in response to your letter, staple it to the original letter and drop both pieces of correspondence in the pupil's record folder. You may want to refer to it later in the school year. Every June in every school district there is at least one parent who protests, "If I only knew he wasn't doing well earlier in the year I would have had him tutored." This is usually in response to a notice that the child is being left back. You can go back to the folder and pull out your letter that has the date and method of transmittal on it.

You can get parent action from a positive letter also. For example,

---

Dear Mrs. La Rocca:

I am so proud of Louis. Ever since you came to school there has been a tremendous improvement in Louis's behavior. There have been no more fights with other children on line and the aides in the lunchroom have noticed a big improvement also.

While Louis does most of his homework assignments, I have noticed that he has not turned in any book reports. Can you talk to him about this?

Again, thank you for your cooperation. Louis has certainly benefited from our little talk.

Sincerely,
(Mrs.) Judy Cantor

Figure 6-4

Notice that the teacher starts out with an attention-getting first sentence that brings joy to any parent. She then praises the parent for the child's improvement without mentioning just what action the parent took. This is a valuable technique. If the parent took little or no action the teacher's letter will flatter her into really doing something about the book reports now that the behavior has improved.

This clever teacher sent the letter home the moment some improvement was shown instead of waiting two or three weeks. Experience has shown her that frequently after a parent comes to school there is a "honeymoon" period between teacher and child. Rather than waiting for the child to revert to his earlier negative patterns, she got the letter in the mail. This cemented the parent-teacher bond. Now, if Louis acts up again, there will be very little resistance on the parent's part to help out (" . . . after that very nice letter").

The use of praise is of great value in getting pupils to "shape up."

examples of reinforcement and shaping

Teacher praise is a form of social reinforcement. It reinforces a positive behavior displayed by a pupil. Social rewards include verbal praise, hugs, kisses, pats on the head, winks, and so on. Nonsocial rewards include tangible items like toys, games, trinkets, pencils or edibles like fruit, nuts, or candy. There are also activity rewards such as extra gym periods, free time, classroom games, movies, helping the teacher, working on projects, etc.

You can deliver reinforcement through tokens in the forms of stars, checkmarks, or poker chips. These are exchangeable for backup rewards. Token reinforcement has the advantage of meeting the individual differences found in your pupils. Some pupils may save up stars or chips to "purchase" an extra snack or more gym time or any other reward that appeals to them. Don't hesitate to use this kind of strategy; if you see that it is having a positive effect on pupil behavior, keep it up.

You have, no doubt, found children who have no idea of the kind of positive behavior you are looking for. They truly don't know what absolute silence is or what sitting still is all about. It appears as if they can't do what you ask. Before you give up on them, try "shaping." This technique begins by reinforcing a form of behavior that may bear only a remote resemblance to the kind of behavior you want. Praise them for the small steps they take in the right direction. Shaping is simply the process of successively reinforcing ever closer approximations to the final forms of behavior desired by the teacher.

Notice that, for the past few pages, we have not talked about punishment. There are many good ways to bring about desired results without being punitive.

how to discipline pupils without punishment

Traditional punishment involves restricting pupils, bringing in the principal, and contacting parents. Many successful teachers are more likely to use positive incentives and encourage pupils to follow desired behavior and develop self-discipline. How do they do this? The answer lies in the use of class involvement and the encouragement of individual problem-solving. For example, give your pupils choices in making rules and also in deciding what sanctions should be applied to offenders. A problem involving one pupil is often shared by the entire class. This helps the pupils find positive answers and helps the class develop empathy and problem-solving skills.

Since discipline problems are best solved when it is known what caused them in the first place, be on the alert for symptoms. When pupils seem inattentive, determine whether they have been sitting too long. Try saying, "Everyone up, let's walk around the room." For younger pupils, a short exercise game or movement activity will perk up attention spans.

Realize that pupils are often capable of solving their own problems. When a youngster uses unacceptable language on the playground, suggest that he work out the problem himself. In many cases the pupil will decide to write a letter of apology to the teacher and peer involved.

You can help pupils help themselves by drawing up contracts. Private conferences are used by many teachers. During such a conference draw up a student contract containing a specific plan to solve the problem. Have the child sign it and you sign it too. Set up a schedule for checking progress and you are on your way.

On your way where? To a wholesome relationship with your pupils who need a little extra attention.

how to cope when things get rough

The Stoic philosopher, Epictetus (first century A.D.), noted that "people are disturbed not by things, but by the views which they take of them." This certainly applies to teachers who work hard all day with pupils who are often reluctant to learn or even to behave. There are times when we react or overreact to things our pupils do or say. We tend to take these things too seriously and too personally. As we have said before, "You are not the target of every aggressive act committed by a pupil in your class." If the best teacher in your school took over your class for the day, she or he would most likely observe the same misbehavior by the same child at the same time. She or he might handle it differently but most assuredly would not be disturbed in a personal way.

This is not to say that you mustn't care. These children are craving caring adults in their lives. We urge you to care and to continue trying these ideas and any other sound practices of your own. It is important to find gratification in the tiny successes rather than to always look for something spectacular.

Keep in mind a rational approach to discipline and control. Say to yourself: "It would be nice if I were perfect and loved by all my pupils. But I'm not—no human is—I don't have to put myself down for being human and imperfect." Or, "It would be nice if the world were a happy, wholesome place with all children secure and eager to learn. But, unfortunately, I don't rule the world." Or, "It is unfortunate and inconvenient when things don't go the way I plan them but it is hardly a catastrophe. I will survive it."

Only by feeling this way will we be able to hold on to good teachers like you. And you wouldn't be reading a book like this if you weren't interested in refining your techniques and becoming a better teacher. There is much talk today about "teacher burnout" and statistics that show many experienced teachers leaving their profession because of incorrigible pupils. Reread the three statements we cited above and carry on.

7

offering second chances as a discipline tool

The wonderful thing about teaching is that every September you have another chance; another opportunity to perfect your skills, improve your techniques and refine your discipline tools. Throughout the school year your pupils need second chances, too. Don't feel in November that it is too late for this term. There are ways to offer your pupils a second chance at virtually any time during the year—as long as you do it right. And that is the subject of this chapter—offering second chances. From the start we would like to point out that this does not mean being lenient or compromising your position in the classroom.

how not to get conned by your pupils

The kids in your classroom are experts. They are expert at sensing any weakness or lack of confidence felt by their teacher. As early as first grade they can tell when a substitute teacher is going to make them work and when they will be able to get away with lots of free time. They can also tell when you are in a bad mood or when they can get you to do almost anything.

It's very important to keep your cool and your distance the first two months of school. We heard one experienced disciplinarian say, "I never crack a joke or try to make my pupils laugh until Christmas."

This is over a rather long period and is perhaps too rigid a rule BUT you should see this teacher in her classroom! The children love her. When they move on to the next school, she is one teacher they want to return to visit. She has excellent control and gets her lessons across with considerable success. All this appears to be done effortlessly, and in a calm voice. She is never conned by her pupils. Of course, there are times when the class gets seductive and tries to cajole their teacher into, "Just one more game, please?" or "Why can't we go to gym like Mrs. Green's class?" You may not feel comfortable with this approach—but think about it.

The easy way out is not always the easy way in the long run. It may be easy to accede to a pupil's request right now. After all, it doesn't cost anything to let Ricky go to get a drink even though you said "no more drinks" a half-hour ago. After all, he is a nice boy and never causes any trouble. One little drink isn't going to make teaching this class any more difficult. Don't kid yourself! Saying "yes" to Ricky may haunt you. For now Marcia wants a drink also. How can you refuse her? ("Our teacher lets the boys do anything they want" you hear her whisper.) Are you going to say "no" to Marcia and give credence to her suspicion that you prefer boys to girls? Are you going to say "yes" and then have all the kids ask for drinks in spite of your ruling of a half-hour ago? By being firm in the first place you can avoid all of this difficulty; and—more important—gain the respect of your pupils for being a teacher who means what she says.

Another way not to get conned is to listen critically to everything your pupils say, especially when they quote another teacher or school official. Of course, it is easier for you to believe your pupils when they say, with perfectly straight faces, "Mr. Broward said we can leave our books home on Field Day." Upon checking with Mr. Broward you may learn that he said that pupils will miss their fourth and fifth period classes on Field Day and they can leave *those* books at home. Your pupils may not have meant to tell a deliberate falsehood; it's just that they would have liked to have heard what they reported to you.

Don't believe everything your pupils say is happening at home. A child may come to class and say that he is moving to another state. Since he is one of your least favorite pupils you want to believe this story and begin to take the pressure off this pupil. After he has gotten away with murder for a few days you find out from his older sister that his parents were thinking of moving sometime next year. Foiled again!

When a pupil comes running up to you crying and through her sobs you learn of some misdeed committed against her in the school yard by Richard, check the facts before you pounce on Richard. The "victim," upon closer examination, may have provoked Richard and may be more to blame than he is.

Yet, in each of these cases, while you insist on probing further in order to get at the truth, you must also let the pupils know that, while you don't buy their story this time, you will give them another chance. Your pupils should go away feeling that, while they didn't fool you, you are not angry with them for trying. That is quite different from the inexperienced teacher who revels in the fact that she caught her pupil in a lie and reminds him of it often.

how to set up a reward system

We know a super teacher who recently retired. She maintained excellent control with the most difficult of classes. A year after her retirement, her youngest daughter began *her* teaching career. Prior to the opening of school our friend gave her daughter a manual on how to train a pet. Needless to say, the beginning teacher was puzzled. "What's this for?" she asked.

"Take my word for it," answered her mother, "start your class off according to the same principles and you will have a happy class in good control." The idealistic daughter was troubled by the parallel and was about to dismiss it as the onset of senility.

But her curiosity got the better of her. She began reading the manual and found the author's theme: "reward appropriate behavior and ignore—or try to ignore—any inappropriate behavior." Sensing some wisdom in her mother's gift, she tried to analyze the principles she read about and applied them to her classroom. As you might have guessed, the results were amazing. The young teacher structured a system of rewards and reaped a harvest of positive control.

Let's look at how last year's teacher handled Willy. Here are some of his behaviors, along with the response that each one evoked:

Behavior	Response
Sticking his tongue out	Scolding by teacher
	Giggles from girls
Doing his individual seat work	No visible reaction from anyone
Hitting classmates in yard	Sent to principal

Let's see how smart you are. Without knowing anything more about Willy, which behavior(s) do you think he would repeat? Why?

If you picked the "tongue" and "yard" incidents you are right. That's just what he did. At home no one paid much attention to Willy. He needed to have someone notice him at school. When he did his seat work no one noticed or recognized him. If he stuck his tongue out or hit a classmate in the schoolyard he got attention immediately.

For Willy it was important to get attention and so to him it was a reward when the teacher or the principal scolded him. These rewards actually reinforced his bad behavior.

But the teacher he had this year had mastered the theories behind the dog-training manual and used behavior modification, even though she didn't know that term. This is what she did:

Behavior	Response
Sticking his tongue out	Ignored by teacher
Doing his seatwork	Teacher praised Willy. She also let him be the book monitor on days that his work was accurate
Hitting classmates in yard	Teacher investigated to see if other children contributed to the fighting

Under this new setup the teacher's verbal praise acted as a positive reinforcer. Because of this, Willy was stimulated to repeat the desired behavior, and at the same time he got the attention he craved.

Part of such a reward system is the negative reinforcer. This is when removal acts as a stimulus for the individual to repeat the desired behavior. When Willy's teacher detains him until the others have gone to lunch, this might be a negative reinforcer and might eliminate his "hitting" behavior; but only if it makes Willy want to go to lunch with his friends enough to make him behave appropriately. Care must be taken so that Willy does not see being detained as a "payoff"—receiving attention from the teacher. By assigning Willy extra work to do while being detained, his teacher removes any idea from his mind that this is a payoff.

case study involving management of group behavior

Miss Ruff was a first year teacher in an elementary school. Her class was the slowest in the grade with five children who were quite disruptive, underachieving, and very difficult to manage. She was engaged in a constant struggle to maintain only a minimal level of control in the classroom. The average rate of talking out, being out of seats, yelling, and class disruptions was quite high when compared to the other classes in the school. The rate of compliance with her commands was less than 50 percent. Miss Ruff felt that the children had little respect for her teaching skills—and she was right.

She continued to rely on verbal reprimands, warnings, and sending children to the office as methods of controlling the class. These techniques were only minimally effective at best. Sometimes they seemed to make the children act out more.

Fortunately, she had a good principal who was interested in working with her. After observing the scene, the principal recommended a group behavior management program for the entire class. This would give every pupil a second chance.

The principal recommended a program that consisted of these steps:

1. Develop a set of explicit classroom rules.
2. Establish a rating system consisting of pluses or minuses based on how well these rules are followed.
3. Follow a systematic praising procedure where the class as a whole and individual pupils would be praised for following classroom rules.
4. Make a daily activity reward available to all class members when the reinforcement of positive behavior is achieved.

This is how it was implemented. A list of ten major rules were developed and couched in simple language. Next, Miss Ruff marked off a column 10 inches wide on the side of the chalkboard. The school day was broken down into 20-minute segments. The segments were listed vertically. Every twenty minutes she awarded the class either a plus or a minus. For example:

Time	Rating
9:00-9:20 AM	+
9:20-9:40 AM	+
9:40-10:00 AM	−

Together, Miss Ruff and the principal reviewed the praise component of the program. In addition to offering praise when due, the principal pointed out another technique: instead of reprimanding a pupil for breaking a class rule, Miss Ruff should praise an adjacent pupil who is behaving appropriately. In this instance, the adjacent pupil becomes a behavioral model for the pupil who is behaving inappropriately. In addition, this procedure shows that teacher attention will be given for appropriate classroom behavior and not for rule breaking.

Finally, the principal and Miss Ruff discussed the group reward system that would be used to back up the rating system. A daily group reward of an activity would be available for meeting the reinforcement criterion. Activity rewards would include games, recess, and other events and activities that the children enjoyed.

With some practice, Miss Ruff made additional refinements and both she and the class got a second chance to improve discipline. For example, at the beginning, Miss Ruff found it best to give the class the benefit of the doubt in awarding ratings so as to increase their chances of earning the group reward and experiencing it. Later on, she realized that she couldn't be too lenient in her ratings. This would teach the children that only a very minimal effort would be necessary to earn the daily group reward and the goals of the program would not be achieved. The program operated quite well for the remainder of the school year. Both Miss Ruff and the pupils benefited by the program.

gaining pupil confidence and support

In order to get something from your pupils, such as their confidence and support, you must give something in return. You must make them feel that you are democratic and that you are giving them a "real piece of the action."

We have put this information in the form of an acrostic. The first letter of each of these items spells out the phrase: NO MISCHIEF.

Inside a responsible, democratic classroom there are:

Normal give and take

Ongoing activities that spark pupil interest

Mutual respect

Influence, not power or weakness

Shared responsibilities

Consequences for behavior, not punishment of bad pupils

Helpfulness, not competition among pupils

Inner desire to learn

Encouragement, not criticism or unconcern

Freedom and order, not dictatorship or chaos

Review this mnemonic device often. Check yourself to see if you are applying the ten principles every day in your classroom. If you are, you will be giving your pupils a feeling of security. They will feel that you are willing to offer them a second chance at any time.

how to use contemporary guidance techniques

Competent teachers everywhere have developed insight into child behavior. This is not theoretical or philosophical thought but rather practical, down-to-earth awareness of child psychology based on daily, face-to-face encounters of every kind. Yet, many teachers are too modest when it comes to their ability to single out the pupil who has an emotional problem, needs counseling, or has a serious learning disability. The psychologist, social worker, or guidance counselor has many highly specialized skills for dealing with these special children. But you, the experienced classroom teacher possess a skill that none of the clinicians have. YOU are an expert in "pupil normality." You and you alone have seen scores, maybe hundreds, of normal children interacting in the classroom situation. You know the bounds of normality. You can spot the child who is atypical because of your experience with the typical child of that age.

Don't sell yourself short. The very nature of your job makes you an expert in how children on a particular age level function. You can see and feel when there appears to be some dysfunction.

Sometimes you are not sure. We would like to share with you some simple guidance techniques that you can use with pencil and paper to confirm your suspicions. Because these techniques all involve writing you can then show your documented evidence to your principal, social worker, or school psychologist.

The Autobiography

You can motivate the writing of class autobiographies by reading brief incidents from the lives of pupils' heroes. Or, the teacher may provide a vignette of an experience or two in her own life. She should briefly sketch a home situation, including the types of information she hopes to find in the pupils' autobiographies. Keep pupils from discussing very personal items that might offend their parents.

A suggested list of items of biography follows. No attempt should be made to gather all this information at one session or in one essay.

Changes of residence
Parents' occupations
Family constellation
Any health difficulties
Recreational activities
What do you worry about?
When were you happiest?

Parents' birthplaces
What do you consider a good time?
What do you like about school?
What subjects don't you like?
Do you like to be alone?
What are your problems?
Who are your friends?

Such accounts furnish pertinent facts to aid the alert teacher toward better understanding her pupils. Unusual autobiographies can be shared with appropriate personnel.

Sentence Completion

Another technique, often used in the field of language arts, is the presentation of the incomplete sentence. One or more short phrases are presented to the pupil and he is asked to complete the remarks. The following are representative of the types of partial statements that have been used successfully.

I feel happy when . . .

I feel sad when . . .

I hate it when . . .

I like people who . . .

I feel ill when . . .

I am tempted to lie when . . .

I was happiest when . . .

When I am unhappy I would like to . . .

When something is bothering me I . . .

The thing that troubles me most is . . .

I wish I could . . .

Responses to the above phrases give information about the fears, aversions, ambitions, satisfactions and annoyances of the children. These can be useful in giving your pupils a second chance at succeeding in school. Don't hesitate to refer a child with unusual responses to a clinician for confirmation.

Word Association

Today, everyone (adults as well as children), is game oriented. To stir up enthusiasm you need only announce, "Today we are going to play a game."

You pupils will look upon the word-association device as a game. The teacher presents a list of words such as the following to the class: *sing, sick, pride, pin, new, habit, pray, money, silly, book, paper, bad, child, speed, glass, doctor, ice, flower, happy, clothing, weed.* The list always includes words having an emotional connotation. The children first write numbers on the page to correspond with the number of words to be read to them. As the teacher reads, they place a word of their own choosing after each dictated word. When checking the lists, the teacher often comes upon strange word associations. In many instances strange word choices have focused attention on the total behavior picture of a child who was in need of clinical help. If you, the teacher, consider a child's word response strange, talk it over with your principal and/or guidance counselor. Remember, you are NOT to play psychologist. This is merely a broad screening device.

Since a child is seen as the sum of his experiences it must be kept in mind that a single response to a single situation can be viewed only in the light of all the other information available about him or her.

ways to handle makeup assignments

It's important for pupils to make up work that they missed because of absence or inattention. It's as necessary for bright children as for average or slower ones to know that what goes on in class is very important and if they don't do the work when assigned, they must make it up. Every day on which a child misses school broadens the continuity gap. He may not have missed much, but he doesn't know it. He fears that unknown quantity. By giving him a second chance to make up the work, you restore his self-confidence. It also enhances your image when the child feels that everything you assign is of some import.

Of course, your reputation for fairness is enhanced when everyone makes up missed assignments. Even if you don't check every word, be sure you go over the work submitted and make some marks on the paper before returning it. Get in the habit of returning pupils' papers promptly. Few things turn kids off more than the teacher who keeps their papers for three or four weeks and then returns them without any comment on them. Worse still is the teacher who collects a major project near the end of the term and doesn't return it at all.

If you teach in the junior high school or in some other departmental setup, it will take class time to check with pupils on back assignments and tests. While this is going on, give the class something interesting to do at their seats. A ditto sheet on unexpected, special material will do. Give directions for the sheet and announce a due date. Usually the freshness stimulates greater diligence than would a textbook assignment with pages written on the board.

recording discipline infractions

Get yourself a marking book of some kind. It can be a commercially prepared type from a school supply house or it can be something you make up yourself. Give it a name that the pupils can recognize like, "my black book," "the red book," "the marking book." Inside, list every pupil in your class. When you notice that the children are getting a little out of hand, just reach for your marking book and silently make some entries. At first you will find yourself writing minuses, "D's" or other negative marks. After a while you will find that merely by opening the book and scanning the list of pupils' names you will have achieved silence in the room.

This kind of ploy can be used with any kind of class. When you have more serious behavior problems you will need to make more detailed records of pupil misbehavior. Allow time along the way for constant evaluation and reevaluation of your programs and strategies. Remember, the pupils' behavior will tell you what you need to know. Train yourself to be observant. In this sense every class provides an opportunity to evaluate the progress of your pupils.

Properly prepared anecdotal records are a must in any program of behavior modification. Knowing how to observe a child and how to record that observation is a skill you will develop with practice. Then you can use that concrete record to draw subjective conclusions concerning a child's adjustment and learning patterns.

Be aware of the atmosphere in which you observe the pupil. Is he engaged in an activity he likes, like gym or shop? Is he in a setting different from the regular classroom? Is this a larger group of pupils, like the lunchroom? Does he have more difficulty in the afternoons?

The procedure you use will vary from time to time. Simply jot down every behavior you see the child engage in. We like listing by phrases. Do not stop to evaluate whether or not a certain behavior is significant. Write it down and decide later. Above all, do not be judgmental. Write down what you observe without any editorial comment. Do NOT try to analyze the pupil's motives or pass judgment upon what he has done.

Column A below lists some fair to poor comments taken from an anecdotal record. In column B we have tried to improve upon the same observation.

Column A	Column B
	bit his lower lip
	threw pen on floor
got angry	shut book and put it in his desk
	played with book cover
wasted time	stared out the window
	used pen to "tattoo" his arm
annoyed others	took pencil from Anne's desk
	made a face at Hal as he returned to his seat
	pushed his desk up against Pete's

summary

Through these pages we have tried to give you some practical ideas for helping pupils get a second chance. We consider these basic principles necessary if a teacher is to change a pupil's behavior for the better. We have also suggested different ways in which you can put these ideas into practice.

The only thing that counts is whether or not it works. Did you solve your problem? Did you change the pupil's anti-social behavior? You may have used some technique exactly as we described it, or you may have adapted it. Great! Whatever works is wonderful!

8

using other personnel to help enforce discipline

Walt Whitman Junior High School has 68 teachers on its staff. In addition to the principal, three assistant principals and a guidance counselor, there is one teacher who serves as the full-time dean of discipline. All behavior problems are referred to him on blue cards. These cards indicate all kinds of infractions of school rules from gum chewing to attempting to strike the teacher.

We asked the dean to prepare two lists for us. One was a tally of the various reasons for the issuing of a blue card during the past school year. Such items as "threatening another student" and "continually interrupting the class" were the leading causes for referral. We asked him to prepare another list with the name of each teacher and the number of blue cards each teacher filed in the past school year. The results were fascinating. Some teachers made few or no referrals. Many teachers averaged one per month. There were some teachers who actually averaged one or more per day!

These blue cards were for behavior problems that the teacher could handle himself in the classroom. One item on the printed card was "steps taken by the classroom teacher to remedy the situation prior to making the referral." Apparently, some teachers were unsuccessful in handling discipline problems themselves.

how to work with school authorities

Some teachers have been trained to take care of their own discipline cases. These teachers feel it is a poor reflection on them if they have to ask someone else in the school for help. Still other teachers feel that "if any kid gives me lip, I kick him out—send him to the dean; after all, that's his job; my job is to teach the kids who want to learn." Who is right? How should you work with the authority figures in your school?

It goes without saying that children are quick to spot the weak teacher. If a teacher continually sends pupils who misbehave out of the room, the pupils will be quick to assess that teacher as not being able to "take care of himself." However, we must also point out that there are occasions when it is best to remove a disturbing child from the room; so be glad that your school has such a resource available. There are also times when, after you have taken steps to remedy a situation, it is best for all concerned to have a third party step in and take over. These need not be automatic face-losing situations for the teacher.

The best way to enforce discipline is to have a moderate approach where the children respect your authority and your standards, but recognize that there is a "ladder" of referral with other steps built-in. Deans have told us that when they get a blue card or other referral from a teacher who rarely asks for help they know that something is wrong and they take care of it immediately. Calls for help from teachers who constantly send in referrals are not handled the same way. This may not be right, but it is human nature to respond in such a manner.

Don't tell a child, "I'm going to send you to Mr. Dean" every time he forgets a pencil. Do insist that the pupils follow your rules; save a referral to the dean for those cases that are repeated offenses or very serious matters (assault or threatened assault).

making the most of your fellow teachers

The sum of the skills of a group of teachers has to be greater than any one individual teacher's. Begin to reach out to your fellow teachers. See if you can t start some form of tandem, team, or departmentalized arrangement. In this way all the teachers can capitalize on each other's strengths.

Many pupils with learning problems find the change from one classroom to another in non-self-contained settings more of an adjustment than they can make. Other, equally difficult pupils will find the stimulation of different teaching personalities just the thing they need. They seem to improve when they don't have to be cooped up with one teacher.

If you are using a behavior modification approach, it is important that you work closely and consistently with one another. When you do this you will more than double the results that you might achieve alone. A bit of communication will bring you all the cooperation you need.

Mike had trouble with fine-muscle activities and grew to dislike his art class. He just couldn't handle it. When his official class teacher explained the situation to the art specialist, she was more than glad to have Mike work on an alternate project that was more satisfying to him.

Sonia was artistic, but her teacher could not stand all the mess involved in creative painting. One of the other third grade teachers had a special interest in art and invited Sonia to attend her weekly classroom art classes—she didn't mind the mess at all. She *did* feel insecure with Marc, who was some kind of science whiz. She just couldn't answer Marc's advanced questions, or give him meaningful work to do. The neat, organized, "no mess" teacher had been a lab technician and was glad to have Marc spend time in her room working on experiments.

In one school, a chart was posted in the teachers' lounge on which such help could be requested in "want-ad" style. Sometimes another teacher's help can also be enlisted to change a child's classroom assignment to overcome a clash of personalities between teacher and pupil or between two pupils.

Some districts employ a reading resource teacher for each school, while others may have one reading coordinator for the entire district. Start by analyzing the specialized help you have right in your building or in your district.

Don't overlook anybody—the Audio-Visual Coordinator may be looking for a way to promote more direct contact with the classroom.

She may be able to supply just the little extra you need to motivate your special group of pupils.

Also, don't overlook the obvious. Perhaps your troublemaker needs glasses, can't hear your instructions, or is suffering from some illness like diabetes. Be sure you begin with a referral to the school nurse or doctor. Make sure the parent follows up with clinic visits. Or if glasses are prescribed, make sure he wears them.

Make sure your referrals are appropriate. If a pupil's behavior problems are really stemming from his noticeable speech defect, it is senseless and inefficient to consult the school psychologist before you have spoken with the speech therapist.

how to remedy the drug and alcohol problem

Pills and booze have been a headache to educators ever since they crept into schoolyards during the permissive days of the 1960s. But these days school disciplinarians say they've got better remedies, and they're not panicky or afraid to use them.

"The panic that used to surround drugs and drinking is not there any more," says Robert DeIulio, chairman of the counseling department of Newton North High School in Massachusetts. "It's one of the many developmental problems facing children. It's just one more problem teachers have to deal with."

Newton police say marijuana use at the suburban Boston high school is as big or bigger than ever, but school authorities are less nervous becuase they have found ways to deal with teens who smoke. The remedies range from counseling programs to police surveillance and frequent suspensions. Teachers and administrators say they're not opposed to taking a hard line anymore.

"One thing we're finding is there are more severe suspensions that are drug-related," says Massachusetts Education Commissioner Gregory Anrig. "We're in a period where there is more emphasis on discipline. Educators are taking a firm stand when it comes to classroom discipline."

If your school is like most, they don't like to emphasize the discipline they employ. Instead, they point to "preventative" education courses and in-school counseling.

To deal with the marijuana problem, some New England school authorities have called on police to stake out schoolyards and to film students between or after class. After the camera catches students believed to be selling, buying or smoking dope, the students' parents are called in to view the film.

The police say they're interested only in arresting the heavy pushers and frequent users. The idea of the film is to stress the seriousness of the situation, however, and not to make arrests.

While most authorities agree that a film would not hold up as evidence in a courtroom because it would be hard to prove the substance is a drug, the procedure has cut down on the use of school grounds as a drug-trading post.

In Warwick, Rhode Island, the police occasionally pose as students—"mostly to get to the people who sell the drugs" says Police Captain Buzz Nelson.

The use of a camera was also tried last year in Portland, Maine, in the small western Massachusetts town of Lenox, and in Marshfield, Massachusetts, on Boston's South Shore. Some teachers feel that this is an invasion of privacy. Advocates say it can be handled confidentially. It works, they say—at least temporarily.

"The kids all admitted using it when they came into the office. All admitted they felt it was not proper, at least not in school. We explained to them what would happen if they were caught and referred to the courts," said Paul Perachi, principal of Lenox Memorial High School.

So you can see that schools are taking a hard line on drugs and alcohol. Statistics compiled by the Department of Education show that among the 12 to 17 year old age group, 28 percent have tried marijuana at least once, compared with 53 percent who have used alcohol. Alcohol is still the Number 1 problem. The difference is that schools are now getting everything out in the open. Teachers are not panicking about drugs. They are reporting its use to administrators who have a much closer cooperating relationship with local police, as we can see from the above examples of staid New England.

getting your principal to help

The head of your school has the unique potential for perceiving and using the strengths exhibited by individual teachers in your building. No one teacher can be a master in all areas. Likewise, even the least experienced teacher has one talent to offer the others.

Your principal can be a catalyst in opening up communication with the entire staff, including custodial, lunch, and auxiliary personnel. Here is an informal list—compiled by a principal we know—of talents possessed by the staff that can help in handling discipline problems within his building. We have included the descriptions in parentheses so that you can see how varied are the staff members he utilizes.

NAME	TALENT
Jim Dunn	Worked as tennis instructor
Jane Bianco	Builds sets for church plays
Mary Smith (lunchworker)	Excellent seamstress
Henry Beaver	Amateur weightlifter
Judy Franz	Owns her own horse
Dave Mateo (janitor)	Builds his own kites
Katy Burke	Uses behavior modification
Marie Keyes	Personalized reading techniques
Rose Volpe (secretary)	Has taught piano
Carol Schuman	Makes math manipulatives
Gerri Garcia	Spent two years working with disturbed children
Dottie Withers (cook)	Part-time gymnast
Helen Kelly	Former child agency intake worker

This list could be extended to include every faculty member. A good principal doesn't necessarily publish such a list but should keep one like it in his head or in his desk for ready reference. The point is that staff members who have a skill or interest that can be tapped to reach a troubled or troublesome youngster should be utilized.

Another way to get your principal to help with your difficult pupils is to find out just what his or her strengths and interests are. Most principals would be flattered if you asked them to share some expertise in an area with your class or some youngsters of your choosing.

Still another way is for the principal to get a successful teacher to describe in detail some technique he or she uses that works. For example, one teacher may be using behavior modification with excellent results. The principal should have that teacher describe what she did or is doing, at a staff meeting. He can also smooth out some of the difficulties that might be encountered by the rest of the staff. It might be difficult for one teacher to tell another that he is reinforcing the wrong behavior in a child. The skilled principal can find a way to communicate this without making the teacher approached become defensive. This is especially important if the matter concerns transferring a child out of a certain teacher's class. Teachers— conscientious ones—like to feel that they can always meet the needs of all students; an unrealistic standard, albeit a noble one.

Your principal, since he or she controls the purse strings, should also allow teachers to order and use any kind of learning materials that they can justify, within budgetary limits.

setting up a mental health team

Behavior problems in your school and your class will never go away by themselves. Some kind of intervention is needed. In some schools, a "crisis intervention room" is set up. This is a quiet, small room (usually a former office) where a pupil with an acute problem can "cool off" for a few minutes or a class period. It must be staffed by an adult. This can be a school aide or a teacher on duty for that period. In large schools, it may become a full-time or half-day assignment for a teacher. This adult should relate closely with the regular teacher so that a team approach is operating. The class teacher may send an assignment with the pupil to the crisis intervention room.

Another very useful way of using a specialist's abilities effectively is to work toward some kind of team approach to behaviorial problems in your school. One elementary school we visited conducted a "clinic" every Thursday afternoon. The following specialists attended these clinic sessions: the principal, part-time counselor, district psychologist, district social worker, school nurse, speech therapist, reading resource teacher, and family assistant. The latter is a paraprofessional who visits the homes and serves as a liaison between home and school. She lives in the community and the parents relate well to her.

The team would look at case studies prepared by teachers as well as referrals to see if they were appropriate. Before a child was referred to an outside social welfare agency, the clinic team would exhaust all school and district resources.

Teachers were invited to come in to discuss pupils. Relevant records would be brought to the meetings and the group would ask the classroom teacher to explain the problem. Team members having some previous experience with the family or with that particular child would share any information or insights. By allowing the teacher to verbalize his problems, and by analyzing these problems in the light of all available information, the team sought to find the probable cause of the child's difficulty. Specific suggestions were given to the teacher so that she did not feel alienated or less effective. Follow-up sessions were scheduled so that progress could be reported. This team approach was later refined to have a rotating chair for a classroom teacher on the team. In this way, every teacher had a chance to contribute suggestions and also see firsthand how the team operated. Surprisingly, the other team members saw that every teacher, regardless of level of experience or training had some techniques or insights to contribute.

Working together, the team and the teacher would try to sort out the child's strengths and weaknesses in order to narrow down the areas for investigation. The psychologist might be asked to observe the child in the classroom; the speech therapist to screen his oral language; the classroom teacher to assess his ability to handle math concepts.

In terms of hourly compensation, this was an expensive meeting for the district to support. But in terms of time, this group was really economical. Much overlapping and unnecessary testing was eliminated. Duplication of service was avoided. Most of all, a very high level of in-service training of teachers and other personnel was provided.

Sometimes, the team realized that the resources of the school and the district were not enough. They realized that they had to turn to outside agencies.

using an outside agency effectively

There comes a time when even the most guidance-minded teacher must turn to an outside agency for help. Even if your school has a counselor, there are some problems that are best solved by an agency. Before suggesting to a parent that they or you initiate the referral be sure you have identified the problem and the need for referral. In order to do this you will need to see the parents often. Be sure you get your principal's approval before you suggest an outside agency.

You can be of great help in simplifying the referral procedures. The parent or parents will probably be afraid to go to a social agency. You can offer such needed assistance as contacting the social worker, helping to fill out the application, answering the questionnaire from the intake worker. At every step of the way, assure the parents that confidentiality will be preserved.

One good technique is to role-play the initial interview with the parents. Make sure they know how to share the pertinent information they have regarding the child. Point up the importance of patience in awaiting outcomes of tests and interviews. Most important of all, stress the need for keeping all appointments. There is nothing more frustrating for a concerned teacher who identifies the behavior problem, gets the parents to accept referral, makes the appointment and then finds out that the parents never kept it.

Your personal contact with the agency often results in more immediate attention to the referral. Whenever possible, the teacher should meet with the agency worker to share information and to plan for the child. An invitation should also be extended to the worker to visit the school so that she might familiarize herself with the school setting and meet other staff members who come in contact with the pupil. Some agencies want to observe the child directly in the classroom.

Feedback and mutual planning will help school and agency understand and implement each other's recommendations.

how to exhaust your resources before you exhaust yourself

Now that you have taken care of the children with problems in your class, what can you do for yourself? The phenomenon of "teacher burnout" is becoming more serious on every school level. We are convinced that there are definite steps that you can take to insure that you do not become another statistic in the growing file of "burnout" cases.

Jane and Joan are teachers in the same school and teach different subjects to the very same pupils. Jane goes home "dead" each afternoon from abuse, frustration, and physical exhaustion. Joan appears to have no such reaction to the day's similar events and personalities. We have analyzed scores of schools and come up with what we call our "ten commandments" to teachers who want to remain "cool."

1. Reduce or eliminate your own response to disturbing stimuli in your classroom. You can't stop the way the pupils treat one another but you can control how you react to this.

2. Refuse to respond to the signal. There are times every day when a youngster will do something "bad" just to get you angry. Fool him by ignoring the signal.

3. Condition yourself for equanimity. When you feel you must do something to stop the bickering or petty annoyances, do nothing instead. Remain quiet and act as if you never heard the curse word or other annoyance. Remain calm and quiet instead.

4. If you must offer a response, delay it. Many things in school can be taken care of later. Think of Scarlett O'Hara. Her philosophy was, "I won't worry about that now—I'll worry about it tomorrow."

5. Protect yourself from disturbing stimuli by maintaining a relaxed posture physically as well as mentally. Be aware of your muscles as you sit, stand, or walk around your classroom. Consciously get them to relax and not tighten.

6. Build yourself a quiet classroom in your mind. You've seen those books about mental golf and mental tennis. Retreat into a quiet, orderly classroom in your mind whenever you think of school. Soon this will become a reality.

7. Build a decompression chamber. Don't rush out of your classroom and into your car every day. Astronauts need a decompression chamber before they return to earth; so do you. Stop in the office at the end of the day and chat with a colleague, the secretary, or the janitor. Make a habit of stopping in the teachers' room to comb your hair or wash your face. This will make the adjustment from your classroom to your home life smoother.

8. Stop fighting straw men. Don't worry about *what if* something happens or that this or that *may* happen. Don't scare yourself to death with your own mental pictures.

9. Make your nerves work for you. Instead of getting jumpy, save your nervous energy for the rare times when a crisis requires extraordinary strength and energy.

10. Develop that winning feeling. Think in terms of possibilities. Tattoo on your brain the idea that you are a good teacher and that *you* are in charge of the class. Develop that idea as soon as you get up in the morning.

Remember this; the self-image you carry around sets the boundaries of what you can accomplish. It defines what you can and cannot do. Expand the self-image and you expand the "area of the possible."

9

making parents
your partners
in discipline

You are not alone in wanting your pupils to behave themselves in school. Parents also want their children to respect authority and learn in an orderly classroom. Why not capitalize on this common goal by making parents your partners and not your adversaries?

Very often, parents get turned off by a teacher's attitude, real or imagined. Their perception of the teacher remains fixed as younger siblings reach that teacher's classroom. It would be in your own best interest to come across as the helping, supportive person you are. Correct any wrong impressions that parents may have by acting in a friendly, concerned manner at school meetings and events. Don't patronize parents or talk down to them. This is the *worst* thing you can do.

Here are some positive steps you can take in working with parents.

how to make a home contact card

This simple 5" x 7" index card can mean the difference between a positive, wholesome home-school relationship and a total lack of communication that is all too often thought of as parent indifference. Get a 5" x 7" index card for every pupil in your classroom. At the top have the pupils put some basic information, such as their name, address, phone number, and names of siblings in the school with their class numbers. If you had just this information for every child and kept it CURRENT you would be on your way. But this is just the first step. After talking to each pupil individually, gather the following data: business address and phone number of each parent, if they work; mother's name if different from the pupil's; father's address, if different; the name and phone number of a neighbor or relative who can be called if the child is sick in school and a parent cannot be located; the name and class of a neighbor's child in the school. For younger children you may want to send a mimeographed letter home requesting that parents supply this information.

You now have a gold mine of information that you can use if a child is sick in school or if he or she misbehaves. No longer will you have to talk about apathetic or disinterested parents who cannot be reached. You now possess many avenues of contact.

Here are more suggestions that successful teachers have used.

On the back of the card jot down bits of information that you have gleaned from talking to the parent at a conference or from the child, such as: *mother goes to work late on Tuesday mornings* (which means you can reach her at home on those mornings), or: *child visits father on the first weekend of each month* (which means you can drop the father a note at the end of each month to report on his child's progress and be sure of a prompt follow-through).

This is also a good place to jot down the name of the social worker if the child is known to an agency or is a foster child. Such confidential information would only be used with the parents' permission.

If space permits, jot down some key items that came up at the last parent-teacher conference so that you have something to refer to before the next conference or phone call.

Such a home contact card can serve as a bridge between you and the parent.

devices for making the most of the telephone

Too often, teachers think of the telephone only as an instrument for telling parents that their child misbehaved in school that day. Here are some positive practices that you can adapt to your situation.

Conduct a telephone "miniconference." Working mothers and parents who have difficulty with transportation can't always come to school when scheduled conferences are held. Why not conduct a miniconference at a mutually convenient time via the telephone? Prepare for the telephone conference by bringing your marking book and a collection of recent classwork papers to the phone. Write down one or two points that you want to get across along with one or two questions for the parent. Don't try to accomplish more than this in one telephone conversation.

Wage a telephone campaign. In Eugene, Oregon, the teachers try to call at least one parent each week to report on the pupil's progress, praise achievement, or discuss a problem. In this way the parents become aware of small problems before they become big ones. Teachers report that a primary value of these phone conversations is that desired pupil behavior is reinforced the same day it happens. Parents in Eugene, Oregon, report that they feel more involved and supportive as a result of the telephone campaign.

Publicize a telephone consultation hour. Send home a schedule of one or two free periods or one lunch hour a week when parents can reach you at school. Advise the school secretary where you can be reached when parents call you at those stated times. This makes parents feel that they can reach out to you whenever there is a problem you should be aware of or just have an occasion to chat with the teacher.

Set up a telephone relay system in your classroom. One parent serves as class mother and she volunteers to have her number duplicated for all the other parents in the class. She in turn chooses four or five parents who serve as "relayers." They, in turn, are given five or six names and phone numbers of parents in the class to call. In this way, if a class trip is planned or suddenly cancelled, the teacher has just one mother to reach, and no one has to call more than five or six parents.

When talking to parents on the phone, remember to use the same guidance techniques that you would use in a face-to-face interview.

writing letters that get a positive response

Gone are the days when the only time a parent got a letter from the school was when the pupil was going to be left back. Foresighted teachers are establishing good feelings with the parents of their pupils with easy-to-do form letters that emphasize the positive or give specific reasons for displeasure before things get out of hand.

For example, you could send out a Progress Letter halfway through the marking period. This should be early enough in the quarter to enable a child and his family to do something about raising his average. We like this one from Evanston, Illinois:

_____3/10_____
Date

Dear _Mrs. Green_,

    I'm your son/~~daughter~~ _Richard_ 's math teacher and I would like to share with you some information about his/her progress so far this marking period. We have taken __4__ tests. _Richard_ earned grades of _65, 70, 55, 70_ %. Based on these grades, his/her present average of test marks is approximately __65__%.

    Of course, this is not the FINAL grade and is subject to change by the end of the quarter. I thought you would like to know his/her current standing so that _Richard_ could bring his/her average up before the end of the marking period. With a little extra effort I am confident he/she can.

                   Sincerely,
                   Albert Quinn
                   Albert Quinn

Please write your comments on the back and return to school.

Figure 9-1

Notice some of the good points in the above letter:

1. It is written in an informal style. It's not stuffy or pedantic.
2. The teacher introduces himself in the first sentence and talks about "sharing information" instead of "I must inform you . . ."
3. This note confines itself to hard data—test grades. It does not mention conduct or attitude. While these frequently go together, you can adapt the letter to suit your needs.

4. The tone is friendly and leaves the door open for improvement. The teacher did not wait until the die was cast and it was too late to do something significant about change.

5. The last line is positive and encouraging.

6. The parent is encouraged to comment on the back of letter and send it to school. Psychologically, by asking the parent to write on the back, or better still, by suggesting that she write comments in the space provided below, you become *partners.* You are saying that the parent's comments are just as important as your own. Also, the piece of paper is not a sacred document from the teacher but a vehicle for exchange. Also, it is less threatening for a parent to write on your paper than it would be to have him write on his own stationery.

Here's a fine letter that focuses directly on discipline.

Dear *Mrs. Brown,*

    A good attitude is school is the key to academic success. This year we plan some exciting learning experiences including trips, independent study, library visits, and guest speakers. Our plans will be wasted unless each child shows self-control. I need your cooperation in getting *Michael* to exercise good conduct in school.

    Every Friday he/~~she~~ will bring home a dated and signed Conduct Slip. If it has "very good" on it, he/~~she~~ has excelled in self-control and no slips will be sent home until further notice. "Good" means a positive effort was made by your child. "Improvement needed" means a definite lack of self-control. The last mark, "unsatisfactory," shows complete disregard for class rules and I will ask that you write a response on the back of the slip.

    Enclosed is the first conduct slip. Please sign it and have *Michael* return it on Monday. Your cooperation is appreciated. You can reach me at school by calling 442-6120 on Mondays at 12 noon.

Sincerely yours,
Louise De Sario
(Mrs.) Louise De Sario

Figure 9-2

Some teachers feel that a pre-printed letter such as the one above is a little too impersonal. Recognizing that a busy teacher can't write an individual letter each time he or she wants to communicate with the home, the following "fill-in" letter combines the best of both types.

Dear *Mrs. White*   :

    I am writing you about *Thomas*   in Class *2/2* Because of your interest in his/~~her~~ behavior in school, I want to tell you about some progress that I have noticed in class: *Thomas is completing his homework.*

    At present, there is still room for improvement. Especially when *he is left on his own. He throws spit balls, calls out and disturbs others.*

    Please write down your comments and have *Thomas* return this letter to me at school. Many thanks.

                          Jerry Meyers
                          Jerry Meyers

Figure 9-3

Notice that this last letter gives the teacher a great deal of flexibility in filling in specific areas of gain in self-control as well as specific discipline infractions. We especially like the way in which the teacher first fills in an example of improvement before he or she points out where there is NEED for improvement. Because the writer of the letter asks the parent for comments, it is likely that these letters will elicit a positive response.

Letters like these should be followed up with phone calls or home visits.

how to make home visits safely and beneficially

In recent years, teachers have been less enthusiastic about making visits to pupils' homes. Sometimes this has been based on bad experiences. At other times it has been dropped as impracticable.

Why not give it a try? By observing some simple precautions, home visits can be safe and beneficial.

In the first place, don't go alone if this is the first visit or you have some doubts about the neighborhood or the kind of reception you will receive. Ask the guidance counselor, reading teacher, attendance officer, school aide, or other teacher to go along with you.

Be sure to call first to arrange the visit. You would not want a parent to ring your bell without calling first. By calling first, you are also able to get the parent's reaction to your visit. Obviously, a hostile parent will make it perfectly clear on the phone that you are not welcome and you will be able to avoid a confrontation at the door.

In Flint, Michigan, teachers routinely visit the homes of their pupils each fall. They report that such an investment in time and effort pays for itself many times throughout the year.

We realize that you will not be able to visit every family. Instead, try to visit every new family. This will really make a youngster feel secure in his new school. You will also have nonthreatening community information to share and this can be a great icebreaker. You may want to try to visit those families that have more than one child in your school. In this way you can go along with another teacher who has another of the family's children in her class.

When you first arrive, concentrate on getting to know one another. Don't begin with a discussion of the best way to teach long division or the need for silence during a reading lesson. Do talk about long-range plans and stress the common goals that you share with the parents.

After a while you can deal openly with a variety of family situations. Avoid belittling terms like "broken home." All children have families—they may have both parents present; one parent living and one dead; one parent absent; they may be children of a single parent, or have foster parents. Don't act surprised or shocked at anything that you are told. Keep the tone of the visit on a friendly, professional level and do not see this as a scenario for a "true confessions" sort of magazine story.

During a home visit you might want to bring up the subject of report cards. Indicate to the parent what your standards are. Also, find out what the parent thinks of the report cards that her youngster has brought home in the past.

how to use the report card for two-way communication

Report cards are highlights in a child's life. Pupils can't help but compare their cards with those of other pupils. These reports also become a source of conflict in the home. Many a forger got his start in life faking his parent's signature on a bad report card.

You can avoid all that and make the report card a two-way street between pupil and teacher and also between parent and teacher.

A few days before you make out the printed report cards, pass out sheets of paper to your pupils and ask them to rate themselves in several critical areas—including conduct. Be sure to explain the marking system your school uses. On the back, have the pupils give the reasons why they feel they have earned that grade. These papers are a wonderful guide for you in making out the printed cards. They also give you insight into how the pupils perceive their performance in the areas cited on the report cards.

If you are not sure of what grade to give a pupil, take another look at how he/she rated him/herself in this area. If it's a close decision why not yield? The pupil is in the process of learning self-evaluation.

If your school district hands out a report card with room for parents' comments, insist that parents write something in that space before returning the card. If the printed report cards do not have adequate space, send home a rexographed sheet that has your child's name and class with large boxes for each of the major report card marks. Insist that parents write a comment in each box and return the form with the report card. In this way, they are reacting to your judgment as indicated by the report card. Study these sheets and refer to them when you make out the next report card.

Schedule some time the week after report cards are given out for "appeals." Let your youngsters and parents know that they can come in to discuss any grade you gave. At the conference table, talk to the parents alone for a few minutes and then invite the pupil to join you. Explain to the parents your rationale in awarding the grade, then listen to the pupil appeal the decision. The youngster is in the process of learning when to conform and when to object, and this could be a crucially important step in strengthening his courage to speak up. This opportunity also teaches the child in vivid terms that the establishment can be reasonable and that speaking up can pay off. Be reasonable in your response and never talk down or act patronizing.

Towards the end of the term, send home to parents a report card that they fill out indicating how much their child has learned in each of the academic areas and also how behavior has improved or worsened. This two-way communication will help you as much as it helps your pupils.

handling the parent-teacher conference

There are basically two kinds of parent-teacher conferences: those set up formally by the school and those called for by you or the parent. Our words of advice apply to either situation, but especially to the former.

Start by encouraging all the parents to attend the Open House and/or the formal parent-teacher conferences. Offer a reward to the pupils whose parents attend. Find out what other times are more convenient for parents who can't attend the Open House and make time for them.

Prepare yourself for a conference by looking over the pupil's cumulative folder. In particular, look for comments made about previous conferences, test scores, health problems, referrals to out-side agencies, etc.

Set up the room in a friendly way. Arrange for two adult-sized seats around a pupil's desk or table. Don't hide behind your desk unless you are expecting a hostile parent and feel you need that security. Check with the office and, if possible, have ash trays, a pot of coffee, some cookies, and a box of tissues near at hand. If it's an afternoon conference, have some toys available for younger siblings who are frequently brought along.

Try not to take notes while the parent talks to you. If you feel you must, offer a pad and pencil to the parents to jot down any suggestions that you make. The key to a successful conference is equality. Remember, you are both adults talking about a child. The parent facing you may not have a degree in education, but does have a great deal of life experience and a vested interest in the subject at hand—the child.

Be as specific as you can be. Have samples of each child's work at hand. Show parents exactly how sloppy, careless, or incomplete the test papers are. Take out your grading book to give examples of grades earned or of homework that was incomplete.

The questions most parents ask are these: "How is my child doing in his schoolwork?" "How is my child behaving?" and "How does my child get along with his/her classmates?" Anticipate some of these questions by telling parents how you perceive their child's relationships in class. Request parent feedback. Frequently the parent can supply the missing piece that you have been seeking in the personality puzzle.

Take the initiative and ask: "Is there any child in the room making your child feel uncomfortable?" Sometimes a parent will mention a name that she would not ordinarily bring up were it not for your question. This is a good way to nip a bad situation in the bud. You can act in a quiet way to remedy the situation.

Use the PNP approach. It stands for positive, negative, positive. Always start the conference with a positive comment about Johnny. For every negative point be sure to suggest a constructive approach to try. Finally, save at least one bit of praise for the child, and end the conference with it.

Encourage a follow-up. Mention that you are available on the telephone and give the school number. Invite them to call—it is rare that a parent will abuse this invitation. Schedule a follow-up interview in a month or ask the parent to call you in two weeks. You may set up a notebook exchange: tell the parent that every Friday you will write a comment or two in the homework notebook indicating improvement in conduct or the need for such improvement.

Invite the parent to come to school unannounced to see just how Ivan behaves in class. This is especially good for the parent who can't believe that things are "that bad" in school. When Ivan gets one or two surprise visits from Mama or Papa he is likely to be less "terrible."

Be lavish with your praise when praise is appropriate. Promise that you will never utter this horrible, trite expression, "You really didn't have to come up, your child is doing well." No thinking teacher would ever say that, yet concerned parents report that they hear this every time they come up for conferences. Instead, say something positive—it should be easy if the child is doing well. Send the parent out of the room glad that she came to school instead of feeling that she wasted her time.

tips for getting parents on your side

Acknowledge parents who are making an extra effort. Are there reading volunteers or class mothers at your school who volunteer their time? Let them know you appreciate their help. Send them a note at Thanksgiving. We know of one parent who kept that note from a grateful teacher on her refrigerator door all year. Ask your principal to acknowledge the contribution these parents are making. This will give you increased credibility in the community. Next year if you have a problem with some disgruntled parent and she complains about you, the complaint is likely to fall on deaf ears for a number of reasons, one of which is that you have already established a reputation that is positive.

Conduct a workshop for parents. Introduce them to techniques you believe they could use to reinforce your efforts in the classroom. Give parents a chance to talk to one another at these workshops. They will get a lot of support from one another when they see how universal childrearing problems are.

Write "love notes" in the pupil's homework book. They might read: "José did better in math today because of the help you gave him." or "I couldn't have managed the class party without your help."

Invite parents as guest speakers or teachers. Perhaps they can teach a native dance or song. Prepare an international lunch one day with different ethnic dishes—some parents can teach the class how to prepare them. Parents enjoy making learning materials under the teacher's direction (games, flash cards, word lists).

When parents feel that they are part of the school team they lose a lot of anxiety. Remember, many parents may have unpleasant associations with schools and teachers. Their own teachers were probably not as enlightened or supportive as you are. You must overcome these negative feelings before you attempt anything else.

a case history

Mrs. Savage is a welfare mother with three children. She was never married and the man she is currently living with is out of work. While her children come to school neat and clean, they are all behavior problems. Mrs. Savage never finished high school and had a "bad record" all through school.

She has never come to parent-teacher conferences and most report cards sent home are lost. There is no telephone number on the school records although the teacher has reason to feel that there is a telephone in the apartment. Notes from school go unanswered.

Miss Smith, the teacher of Mrs. Savage's fourth grader, is very persistent. She contacted the public agency that provides welfare services. She teamed up with the social investigator, and visited the Savage apartment to present Mrs. Savage with a packet of "Good Work" papers and a few pages from the workbook that the fourth grader had not done because of absence. By starting with something positive (the Good Work papers), and getting into something specific (the workbook pages), the teacher was able to build a tentative bridge between school and home. Mrs. Savage was impressed with the teacher's interest and from then on took a greater interest in her children's work. The image of a harsh, uncaring teacher from her own childhood began to fade. This may not have been a correct assessment of her own teachers but nonetheless the child's teacher had to overcome it.

Good luck to you as you reach out to make parents your partners.

10

focusing on self-discipline instead of fear

Almost anyone with a weapon can get another person to do whatever he wants him to do. A mugger with a gun, a lion tamer with a whip, or a teacher with a threat of failure (the dean, or a phone call to the parent), can affect *some* compliance. In this chapter our focus will be on how to get pupils to discipline *themselves;* how to get them to do the right thing because they *want to* and not because someone is holding a weapon over them.

As you think of some of the worst-behaved pupils in your current class, you probably fear that nothing will get them to employ self-discipline. Take heart. Hundreds of teachers with classes like yours have succeeded in instilling a measure of self-discipline in their pupils. We have some of their secrets and we are going to share them with you.

how to restore self-esteem

People, of any age, can't discipline themselves unless they feel good about themselves. The first step in self-discipline is self-esteem. Naturally, you can't tell the bully who threatens other children all of the time, and the teacher some of the time, that you think he is just great! But there are ways that you can provide a positive environment that will enable every child to find something good about himself and his school environment. School or class pride will lead to pride in one's accomplishments and positive deeds. Here are some ways in which some outstanding teachers in New Jersey talked about building self-esteem in disturbed and disturbing pupils:

1. Be fair and consistent. Pupils must learn that they have to be accountable for their own behavior—use isolation and time-out places when necessary. Let everyone know that you play no favorites.

2. Help pupils realize that with freedom comes responsibility. Try to give kids opportunities to make some mistakes. But also hold them accountable for the decisions they make. Show them that they can't blame their parents or teachers for their classroom behavior. They have to realize that it is their own responsibility.

3. Try to roll with the various changes that affect your school. Don't keep thinking about the classes you had years ago. Ethnic groups, economic levels, community needs—ALL change in a school over the years. Good teachers relate to these changes and accommodate themselves rather than dwell in the past.

4. Emphasize basic skills. It's important to touch again the bottom line—how much academic progress does each child achieve? Require hard work of your pupils. Be sure homework goes home and is signed by parents. Give spelling tests, insist on memorization of facts, reteach skills that pupils haven't mastered. Pretest all new pupils for reading placement in a group as close to their talents as possible.

5. Use positive reinforcement techniques. For example: call your kids "All-Stars" because that implies the best, and they will try to live up to it. Depart from the normal procedure for attendance or conduct cards. It's hard for a kid to wait a year to get a perfect attendance or good conduct award, so give them out every nine weeks or two months. They say the same thing as the year-long one does, but with different colors for each nine-week period. The kids love it and attendance and conduct will improve. All kids like to be winners.

6. Get the most out of assemblies. Make sure that every child is on stage at least once a year to sing, take a part in a play, or do some choral speaking.

7. Allow kids to get up and move about. Create learning centers for them. Take them on field trips because much of what they learn happens outside the classroom. Hold a read-in one afternoon a week

for 15 or 20 minutes prior to dismissal time: everyone stops what he is doing, including the teacher, and reads silently; any reading material that the pupil or teacher is interested in is O.K.

8. Make good use of your school's monitorial squads. Push to see to it that your kids are included on the safety patrol, chosen as crossing guards, kindergarten monitors, etc. If they don't live up to the school standards they must step down. But give your kids the chance to succeed.

9. Communicate! Keep the lines open for pupils to talk to you each day. Set aside a conference time in the morning and encourage children to come to your desk for a private chat. Allow a pupil to remain in the room with you when the class goes to a special activity like library or gym. Place a shoe box on your desk where pupils can deposit notes to you on any subject, signed or unsigned. Answer notes when it is appropriate for you to do so.

10. Hand out a supplementary report card. Explain in clear language to the parents just how and why their children are doing as well or as badly as they are. Then they will know whether their kids are ahead or behind. Don't use obscure language or euphemisms. Be direct. Be lavish in your praise if any improvement is noted. Let parents know if there is something about the situation that they can help with.

These ten suggestions have worked for others in building a sense of self-esteem and class pride in pupils who never had either in their past school experiences. This is the first step in self-discipline.

how to help pupils appreciate their uniqueness

Do you accept your pupils as they are? Do you appreciate their differences? Do your kids feel that their teacher accepts them for what they are even if what they are differs from the norm? Do your pupils feel it is O.K. to be different from the boys and girls they read about in their basal reader?

Through the years we are sure you have found that some pupils lead rather bizarre lives outside of school. Some of their home situations are stranger than fiction. Their lives are different from your own childhood or from your own children's lives today. Yet, we must accept them and consider them to be of genuine worth and able to learn, provided there is no abnormality present.

In order to understand themselves better, pupils must "know where they are coming from." Many different patterns make up a family unit. It's fun to see how many there are in one classroom. Before doing this activity, stress that a family unit consists of an adult (or adults) taking care of any children who may be in the family unit. These children may be natural, adopted, or foster children. It is important for children to know that the pattern does not have to consist of a mother and a father, as long as a caring, benevolent person is present.

From this you can move on to the family tree. Kids enjoy discussing their family trees and homes. This gives them an opportunity to discover more about their background, the music, food, and other customs that are part of their heritage. Heredity and environment are discussed through stories and examples of twins separated at birth so that children can see that they are a product of both.

All children, especially acting-out children, need to recognize and identify various emotions. You can use pictures from magazines and/or stories that depict various emotions. Have pupils use their own words to describe the emotions depicted in the illustration or in the story. Help them to see that it is not "wrong" to feel the various emotions but the important element is the way they deal with the emotions that are experienced.

From this discussion you can move on to feelings. They discover, from your leading statements, the types of things that make them sad, happy, angry, and so on. You, the teacher, should also ventilate your feelings. By "rapping" in this way, your pupils will feel freer about discussing their feelings and expressing them. They will also begin to see you as a feeling, caring person and not merely as a corrections officer.

In the area of art you will find opportunities to help your pupils appreciate their uniqueness and the worth of themselves and everyone else in the classroom. Don't ask pupils to look at a painting or scene and then reproduce it. Instead, ask questions like: "How does the picture make you feel?" You will be amazed at some of the replies. Your pupils will be surprised at how each one will get a different message from the picture. Discuss with them the frequently heard expression, "Different strokes for different folks."

You can extend the value of your private conferences with pupils in your class if you ask them to keep a journal. This is a way of immediately releasing feelings. When a child puts feelings down on paper, they are out in the open and he is in a better position to deal with them. It also helps in self-understanding. Since it is not always possible to talk with the teacher when she is needed, this is a way the child can communicate immediately with the teacher. It is also a way to keep up communications after the private conference has ended.

how you can foster individual self-control

The adage, "The apple doesn't fall far from the tree," applies to self-control. Unless you come across as a poised, self-assured person in control of yourself, your pupils are not likely to display self-control, either. Each pupil in your class must learn to govern himself, accurately appraise his own conduct, and understand how important his own conduct is, before he can be a real asset to group self-control.

Children need graphic representations before they can handle abstract thoughts. In teaching math you show them that three things and two things add up to five things before you ask them to add 3 + 2 in their heads. So it is, too, with self-control. Use a chart to show your pupils how they are doing in the area of self-control. Hang a chart with pockets on a wall. Print each child's name on a colored card and insert it in a niche. When a child misbehaves, ask him to remove his card. Remember, the pupil must do the removing, not the teacher. He then hands it to you. You date the card, note the infraction and store the card on your desk. On Friday, every child whose name card is still on display may get it and paste a star after his name. This event can become the highlight of the week. Your kids will look forward to it. On Monday, everyone gets a fresh start. Each pupil whose card is in the teacher's desk replaces it on the chart himself. This system works best after you have established control. You certainly wouldn't start off with it at the beginning of the year before you have established discipline in your class. It is excellent for refining and reinforcing good conduct.

Another more concrete way to foster individual control is to have a system of points. Tell your pupils that, in order to get a passing grade, or in order to move on to the next class, they must earn 1,000 points. Every pupil starts out with zero points. As they show some special effort they get a commendation card with a "ten point" or "twenty-five point" box checked off. When they do something that requires immediate punishment, a "Deficiency Card" is used. Here, too, either ten or twenty-five points are deducted. The number of points added or subtracted depends on the severity or merit of the deed. In addition to the card issued, you, the teacher, must keep a tally in your marking book. With some classes you may want to keep a chart with each child's name and the number of points earned alongside the name. Here is a sample Deficiency Card:

DEFICIENCY CARD

Pupil's Name: Class:
Date:
Reason:

Points Subtracted   ___ 10   ___ 25

Teacher's Signature:

Figure 10-1

Of course, a Commendation Card will be even more effective because it exerts a positive influence. Its format is quite similar.

ways to express encouragement

It is the child who seems to deserve praise least who usually needs it the most. His very low opinion of himself causes him to be especially sensitive to false flattery. You must choose your words carefully when addressing such a pupil. If you get too flowery he will tune you out. Yet, if you don't show some praise he will get discouraged. It is usually not enough to repeat the everyday "good" or "excellent" with such pupils.

We have gathered some techniques that other teachers have used to "turn on" pupils who are easily "turned off" by school.

Start out by using short phrases instead of single words; for example:

I knew you could do it.
Now you have it.
That's better than ever.
I wish I had thought of that one.

There will be times when just part of a test paper or answer sheet will be correct. Be positive. Call attention to the two correct answers in the arithmetic work rather than the eight that are incorrect. Say something like:

You did the first two perfectly.
Use the same technique on the rest.
You are on the right track now.
A little more attention to details and you'll get them all right.

You may want to make some general comments like:

The second time will be better.
That's coming along just fine.
I see you are on the right track.
You've really been working hard today.
I've never seen anyone improve as quickly.
One more time and you will have it down pat.

After building up some self-esteem, don't feel shy about using one word expressions with zip, such as:

Super . . . Spectacular . . . Tremendous . . .
Sensational . . . Fantastic . . . Marvelous . . . Perfecto . . .
Superb . . . Outstanding

It's not uncommon to see a pupil flush with excitement when you use such words of praise in connection with something he has done or said. Many of these pupils never get a word of praise at home. If there is any justification for it, be lavish in your praise; remember, success breeds success.

Take advantage of this opportunity to introduce other cultures and languages. Discuss the ways other people say "very good." Suggest that the class contribute to the list by asking family members who speak other tongues. Write on the board:

Très bien	–	French
Muy bueno	–	Spanish
Sehr gut	–	German

After a while you will see evidence of the pupils mimicking you in offering praise to one another. They will use variations of their own for "very good." At this point you will know that you have succeeded.

You'll find that your kids will show more respect for one another as well as for themselves after they acquire the vocabulary of praise.

a great way to reduce hostility

Let's face it. Many adults resort to fear tactics when they want to control children. Parents, teachers, policemen—all authority figures—are guilty of this. Sadly, these fear tactics beget hostility on the part of the children and the vicious cycle is formed.

If we want to develop self-discipline in our pupils instead of fear, we have to de-fuse this hostility toward adults. Even though we ourselves are not guilty of using fear to get compliance, in the eyes of "problem children," who have encountered many adults using fear, we are equally suspect.

A good way to de-fuse these volatile feelings is to use the technique of interviewing. We don't interview the kids; they interview us. The object is to have the pupils begin to see the adults around them in a different light. The goal is to get the pupils to see the adults who run the school (teachers, administration, aides, bus drivers) as they were as children. The fact that all these adults who run the school were once children and had the same kinds of concerns and problems the pupils are having themselves, make them more accessible.

Most pupils don't know how to conduct an interview. Help them out by recalling some interviews they may have seen on television or interviews they may have read in a newspaper or magazine. It's very important that you do some preliminary interviewing within the class before your pupils venture out on their own. Through such practice, pupils realize how important it is to be prepared to ask interesting questions and learn how to follow-up leads. Some hints you may give them include:

1. Avoid questions that can be answered with a "yes" or "no."
2. Make your questions simple and easy to understand.
3. Listen carefully to the answers.
4. Look for clues in an answer that might lead to a good follow-up question.

5. Write down things that you are afraid you may forget.

It is more efficient to send out groups of three "reporters" to conduct the actual interview with the principal or other adult figure in the school. Remind pupils to make an appointment first. Older youngsters can go along with tape recorders and instant-developing cameras. They might even ask ahead of time if the interviewees could bring to school pictures of themselves as children.

Now for the heart of the technique—the questions themselves. Your pupils will want to ask questions of their own choosing. The following are merely suggested as guides to bring out fuller interviews.

> What is your earliest childhood memory?
> What kinds of games did you like?
> How did your parents treat you?
> What kinds of things did they do with you that were enjoyable?
> What did you do that sometimes disappointed your parents?
> What advice did your parents give you that has helped you the most?
> What did your parents do to you that you would not want to do to your own children?
> How did you behave in school?
> Do you think things are better or worse for kids in school today? Why?

You will be amazed at how much your pupils will enjoy interviewing the adult authority figures in their school. What's more, they will begin to see these people as fellow human beings who are concerned about making school a pleasant place to live in. They will begin to see adults as "real" people who once went through the stresses and strains that they are facing now. The element of fear will begin to fade and the aspect of self-control and self-discipline will emerge.

use the depth approach

This is a technique that is designed to reach a youngster's deep or subconscious mind so that you begin to appeal to him on a deeper level than just compliance. The advertising industry uses this approach all the time. Soap manufacturers don't sell soap anymore—

they sell soft hands. You don't buy vitamins—you buy health and vitality; nor do you just buy transportation when you buy a car—you buy prestige, or fuel economy.

Here are some concrete examples of how others have used the "depth approach" to develop self-discipline.

"I'm looking around for two pupils who are dependable to help Mr. Rinehouse in the office tomorrow." The fourth graders know that helping Mr. Rinehouse distribute supplies is fun and beats classwork, especially when he usually rewards his monitors with a box of colored pencils. They also know that what their teacher means by dependable is someone who follows the class rules to the letter. You can be sure that by the end of the day there will be many "candidates who threw their hats into the ring."

In this example, the teacher appealed to a deeper level than merely asking the pupils to "do their best today." She appealed to their desire to achieve status and recognition.

"This next math problem is not in the book," said Mrs. Landry, "and I'm not sure many of you will be able to do it." She then proceeded to dictate a verbal problem that had every pupil thinking. Because she set it apart from the others and appealed to her pupils' deeper level and need for recognition, she got everyone to put on his thinking cap.

There is no need for you to memorize the wording of these approaches. What's more important is that you remember to appeal to the basic needs and urges that all pupils have: recognition, approval, status, belonging. After some practice, you will be able to use some of these basic needs in reverse. For example, every pupil has a need for recognition. To him, as to all adults, the sound of his name is gratifying and produces a warm feeling. To use it in reverse is to say: "Will that boy in the corner return to his work, now?" Because he stopped his work to fool around, this boy lost his status with his teacher. She even forgot his name. He became a nameless, stateless person; a man without a country or passport. The only way back to recognition is for him to do the right thing. All of this was conveyed when the teacher substituted "That boy" for "Michael." She used the depth technique to reach him on a deeper level. Try it and watch it work for you.

how to develop value awareness

Kids are people. They have values. These values may not be the same as yours. Instead of trying to get your pupils to give up those things that are important to them, try to make them aware of your "adult" values.

A good way to do this is to develop effective thinking; more specifically, ways of solving problems. Everyone has problems. How we go about solving our problems is what separates the successful adult from the failure. You can relate this to your pupils by getting them to think about a mystery story they read or saw on TV. Explain that the steps that their favorite detective used to solve a murder are the same processes that adults use to solve some of the mysteries of life.

Help your pupils supply the rationale for the five steps in the problem-solving process:

1. Gather the facts.
2. State the problem clearly.
3. Brainstorm for possible solutions.
4. Make a hypothesis (select a possible solution).
5. Test the hypothesis (does the solution work?).

Teaching the problem-solving process, then, provides the kind of experience necessary for the mental development that makes real value identification possible.

Encourage your pupils to apply these steps to their personal problems as well. The pupils can brainstorm and list the options open to them.

The feeling of knowing what to do, how to begin, gives pupils a sense of what value awareness is all about. If our goal as teachers is that of promoting feelings of self-worth and self-discipline, this is an effective way to do it. This will give our pupils the means of becoming independent and effective in dealing with problems that will arise when they are not under our care.

In this chapter we have tried to give you some examples of ways in which you can develop self-discipline in your pupils. A tension-free atmosphere with an absence of fear and reprisals will lead to a healthier environment for pupil and teacher.

11

employing simulations that enhance discipline

By playing games—house, school, doctor—the young child learns about life. He or she apes the adult world in his or her own. But our culture provides few such opportunities for older children to pretend or make believe. This is too bad. More and more teachers are focusing on the nonacademic aspects of a child's growth and are introducing activities that deal primarily with psychological development. Such programs are generally called humanistic or affective education. They aim chiefly at enhancing self-concept, increasing motivation, and improving behavior in school.

This chapter is full of games and improvisations that will allow your pupils a simulation of themselves. While they are real and produce real emotions, their tightly-defined limits provide a way to try out new behavior without losing face. These activities have been tested in dozens of classrooms and can easily be adapted to your particular situation.

We will begin with an activity that is probably familiar to you—role-playing.

how to get the most out of role-playing

Role-playing is effective because, through its presentation of social situations and problems, it evokes class discussion. Each participant portrays his role in his own way; action and dialogue varies with each group of performers. You might even have different groups of youngsters in your class act out the same situation. Each group will give it different nuances. The teacher will gain insight into her group from the pupils' choices of roles played. Also, the group response to the participants will tell you how the class feels about role-playing.

This tool helps the participants to interpret their environment, to straighten out conflicting elements, and, most important of all, to understand themselves in relation to others. If you are not experienced in the use of role-playing we suggest you keep the following in mind:

1. Select problems that have some degree of conflict.
2. How the player feels is more important than what he says.
3. The audience must realize that a role enactment is merely an enactment.
4. Caution the class not to interpret literally what they see and hear. They must not judge the person playing the part.
5. Implicit in the situation there must be a specific point which will provoke discussion.
6. The situation should introduce a problem. It does not offer a solution.

When the role-playing is completed, it is your job to encourage spontaneity. You should be sensitive to the best point at which to cut off the action and start the discussion. You can get spontaneous reactions if you ask questions like:

Were the roles sincere?

Could this have really happened?

Does it sound familiar?

Did the players feel the parts?

What other problems were opened up?

What could have been added to clarify the problem of the role?

You can reduce behavior problems by using this technique. In addition, role-playing will help the pupils learn how other feel and why they act as they do. They will begin to detect differences in

values. Role-playing will show them what makes other people "tick."
It will encourage cooperation in solving controversial questions. Also,
role-playing will help bridge the gap between belief and behavior,
verbalization and action. By engaging in this activity your pupils will
increase their spontaneity and be able to experience some release of
tension.

how to master the technique of improvisation

Your pupils, like children everywhere, have a picture in their
mind's eye of themselves as the star of the show. Just think of some of
the antics they pull in class! This is usually supported by giggles of approval from the less courageous pupils. But when it comes down to
speaking before large groups, even the most brazen child becomes
shy.

We've found a method that releases some of these shy feelings
and gives pupils a positive, nonthreatening way to get peer approval.
It's called improvisational drama. You can have children feeling
secure from the start—and that security comes from a bag of props.
Here's how to have your children acting and reacting in ways that you
will approve of:

1. Begin with some warm-up activity. For example, try
charades.

2. Divide the class up into small groups of five or six. Mix the
pupils by having them count off, the ones forming one group, the twos
forming another group, etc. By using this random selection you will
prevent unnecessary bickering about who will be with whom and the
emphasis will be put where it belongs—on the creative aspect.

3. Prepare bags of props. Each bag should contain six simple but
incongruous props, (a pipe, a book, a scarf, a pair of knitting needles, a
tea kettle, etc.) The contents of each bag should be different.
Distribute the bags, one to each group.

4. Ask the pupils to keep their bags closed until they've been
given further instructions. (Later on, you can have the pupils bring in
the kinds of props they would like to see used.) Before the pupils open
the bags, give the following simple instructions:

"Using as many or as few of the items in these bags as you wish,
make up a short skit about five minutes long."

"You will have only four or five minutes to work together in making up the skit."

"Your skit should have a beginning, middle, and an end. Be sure you know how to end your skit."

"Try to think of a simple conflict for your skit. It may deal with home or school situations."

5. At this point, ask the groups to open their bags and use the props in them to create their skits. Do not give the pupils more than five minutes. If you do, they will get involved in a three-act spectacular or else fight about how it should end. In an earlier lesson, explain that they should include WHO they are, WHERE the action takes place, WHAT their goals are and major obstacles that block their goals. While the pupils do the skits themselves, you should act as timekeeper.

6. Prepare the class for the first improvisation. Emphasize that what counts is the process and not a polished performance. Don't interrupt the actors for any reason except for an occasional, "Louder please," or "One minute left."

You'll find that the pupils' nervousness about performing is somehow magically displaced onto the props themselves. In a sense, the props almost become another character that says, "Use me any way you like. I am under your control." The props also give the pupils something to do with their hands.

Of course, there are exceptions to this total involvement. If a child does not want to get involved, don't force him. Some pupils, for any number of reasons, just won't. They'll stand or sit on the sidelines. Leave them alone. The worst thing you can do is force them to join in. Happily, most of these youngsters eventually do participate.

An excellent warm-up activity is something called "The Stick Game." It's a game of free association designed to stretch the children's imaginations to get them to think in the abstract. Thinking in the abstract is something that inner city and suburban children with discipline problems have difficulty with. They appear to be so caught up in the here-and-now that they can't deal with abstract concepts. This game will help.

All you need is a chalkboard pointer or yardstick, something every classroom contains. Hold up the stick and ask, "What can this stick be?" You want them to stretch their imaginations and to form an image of the stick as something else. Walk up and down the aisles handing the stick to each pupil. Each pupil holds it in a characteristic way and tells the class what he has turned the stick into. The possibilities will stagger your mind: a sword, a pogo stick, a golf club, a canoe paddle, an arrow, a rifle, a broom, etc. Be patient; some pupils will take a minute or two to think of what they want the stick to become. Some pupils will merely ape another classmate's description.

This will convince you that there are ways to reach some of your unreachable pupils through games or other nonacademic devices. On the surface, these activities appear innocuous. With careful handling on your part you can turn them into methods of teaching self-control.

ways to acquire skill in gamesmanship

You can help your pupils uncork angry feelings and build positive feelings through the use of these simple games.

How a youngster feels about himself has a great deal to do with how he functions in your classroom. These games will help your pupils look into themselves and learn to accept both criticism and praise from others.

Paper bag games:

You will need several small mirrors (metal ones are best, they don't break), small brown lunch bags, and crayons. Each pupil examines his face in a mirror and then draws it on the side of a bag, including as many characteristics as possible so that if others had to guess who it is, they could. When finished, play a guessing game, talking about clues used to guess correctly. Save the bags for a future activity.

Form a circle. Ask pupils to look in the mirror and pick out one thing they see that they like about themselves. Direct them to give an "I like" statement. If a child can't think of anything, ask other pupils to help him. This works well if the teacher starts with an "I like" statement about herself—"I like my brown hair." Talk about how everyone felt when saying something nice about themselves in front of others.

Return to brown lunch bags. Discuss with your pupils the point that up until now they have done a lot of thinking about facts.

Distinguish between facts and feelings. Ask them about the feelings they get about a person by just looking at his face. In order to relax the pupils, ask them to hold up their paper bag faces and ask the class to comment on the kinds of feelings each bag/face evokes. Point out that the facts about a person may differ from the original feelings.

Face-saving Game:

Cut out a child-sized face from a piece of construction paper. Draw a simple arc to show a smiling face and a suggestion of eyes and ears. All the faces can look the same, or if you or your children are talented enough, you can personalize the face. Each day select one pupil to be the "Pupil of the Day." On that day, his or her paper face is put on the chalk board. Discuss with the class what a "positive statement" is and brainstorm several. Now ask the class to give you positive statements about the "Pupil of the Day" and you write them on the chalkboard. For example: "Dick always shares." After you have elicited six or seven good ones, stop. Remove the paper face and ask the authors of the positive statements on the board to copy them onto the paper face. Add the face to your "Hall of Fame" in the rear of the room. After it is on display for a few weeks, send the face home. You will notice how carefully the youngsters care for their faces. Parents have been known to save them for years. This can easily be adapted to "Pupil of the Week." Your skill comes into play when you select the pupil who most needs this kind of boost to his ego.

All Sizes Game:

Divide your class up into small groups of three or four pupils. Have them weigh and measure one another. Place the results on a large piece of oaktag. Compare likenesses and differences. Discuss the advantages and disadvantages of each. "Mary is tall enough to reach the top shelf in the library." "Juan is short enough to get into the movies at children's prices." Keep the atmosphere accepting of all differences, always directing thinking toward the positive.

Have the pupils fold a piece of drawing paper exactly in half. Ask them to draw two pictures of themselves. The left hand side should be a self-portrait as accurate as they can make it. The right side should be a picture of how they would like to look five years from now. When this part of the project is finished, ask the pupils to cut their papers in half. The fun begins when pupils are asked to match the two portraits after they have been mixed up by the teacher.

These games will help your pupils gain self-confidence because they emphasize positive qualities that every child possesses—even the worst monster in your class. They will begin to see themselves as worthy individuals. We would now like to discuss how pupils can interact more positively with one another.

making sense out of laws in a democracy.

We have talked a great deal about class rules. These can be drawn up as early as Kindergarten. An activity that gives credence to the need for rules and laws is one in which you show how their parents and other adults must follow various rules and regulations.

Begin with rules at home. Ask questions like, "What are some special rules in your family?" "Are there any you dislike because they seem unfair?" "Can you ever dislike a rule that is fair?"

Ask your pupils how they would run their future families. Set up a panel of pupils pretending they are parents. You act as host or moderator of this panel show and ask pupils what they like and dislike about their children and their behavior. You might want to share some of your own childhood experiences and compare notes on family rules prior to the panel show to "warm" them up.

Point out to pupils that the need for certain laws changes through the years. Sometimes laws made long ago that are no longer necessary can be amusing. For example: it's illegal for a donkey to sleep in a bathtub in New York; in Hawaii it's illegal to insert pennies in your ears; or, owning a dog more then ten inches high was once forbidden in Boston. Promote some research on the part of your pupils by having them look for other such anachronisms in the school library.

Ask the pupils to bring in a local phone book. Help them find the telephone number of the appropriate agency to report:

A landlord who does not take care of his tenants' safety

A factory owner who pollutes the air

A neighbor whose dog messes up your lawn

A storekeeper whose scale does not read zero when empty

Whether it is a class rule, a city ordinance, or part of the U.S. Constitution, all citizens, young and old, must be active participants in a democracy. Point out how voters can change laws. Make the pupils feel they are part of the rule-making process in your classroom.

contracting for conduct

Sometimes you can accomplish more if you individualize your reward system. In teaching responsibility and the need for following rules, most pupils can see the group's need to conform. However, some pupils can't relate to a group need or goal and need individual reward systems.

Everyone knows what a contract is. Teachers have contracts; marriages are based on them; workers who are remodeling houses have them. In this age of positive reinforcement you can improve conduct patterns by drawing up and signing a contract with an individual pupil in your class.

As in all contracts, they are only pieces of paper unless both parties abide by their provisions. What makes them especially suitable for a teacher who wants to improve the discipline in her classroom is that they have great appeal to pupils. They reach many pupils who have not been reachable before. One reason is that they are ego-boosting. The youngster who has been "turned off" by school teachers in the past is now the center of attention on a document signed by only the teacher and himself.

The contract is specific and it is written in language the pupil can understand. This, too, appeals to youngsters. Because of its personal nature, contracts are usually kept confidential. This also appears to appeal to boys and girls—every child loves a secret. This takes on the appearance of a private agreement between pupil and teacher. Because it is signed by both parties it gives the feeling of mutual trust. A sample contract is shown in Figure 11-1.

Let's analyze this sample contract. The general tone is positive. The first sentence spells out its main objective—improved behavior in class. The second sentence is quite specific; there is no confusion in the pupil's mind as to what improved behavior means. The second paragraph describes what steps the teacher will take. While many contracts do not refer to a parent or other third party, this one does.

SAMPLE CONTRACT

I, John Russo, agree to improve my behavior in class. I promise not to call out answers, get out of my seat without permission, or crack jokes in class.

My teacher, Ms. Newmark, will give me a new page in her marking book. All of the foolish things I did last quarter are forgiven. My seat will be changed. Ms. Newmark will let my mother know each Friday if I have improved. She will only send home a compliment. If I did not earn any compliments that week she will not send any note home.

In four weeks we are going to go over this contract at a conference. If I improve it will be renewed. If I don't improve I may have my class changed.

(signed) John Russo
(signed) Mary Newmark
Date signed

Figure 11-1

This aspect can be inserted or left out depending on the particular situation. Here, a positive aspect is highlighted once more. A note will go home only if the teacher has something good to report. By prior agreement the parent should be informed so she will know that if no note is sent home it means that something went wrong that week.

Notice that in the last paragraph a time limit has been set up. This keeps the contract fresh. John knows that he has four weeks in which to prove himself—or more specifically, *im*prove himself. A personal conference between pupil and teacher is referred to. This particular contract has a mild threat added at the end. Some teachers feel that this helps "seal" or "notarize" the contract. You may find that it is not necessary and not consistent with your general philosophy. Again, the choice is yours. We include it to give you an idea that you may accept or reject.

While most contracts are kept confidential, you may want, on occasion, to get the pupil's permission to send a copy home. You must get the pupil's feelings about this first.

Through the use of the contract your pupils will also gain an appreciation of the teacher's role in the classroom.

ways in which pupils play teacher

You can alleviate management problems by setting up a pupil leadership program that puts pupils in the role of "teacher." The system is a takeoff on the idea of playing teacher. It gives pupils an opportunity to lead small groups within the classroom. Only after this has been done successfully should you try to have pupils take over the entire class.

Because some of the children will be taking on a great deal of the responsibility for their own learning you will be free to work more intensively with the rest of the class. You can afford now to spend time on individualized instruction or conduct conferences with pupils about contracts.

The small groups led by pupil-leaders cover assigned work that has been reviewed by the teacher. Some of the subject areas are: art, math drills, reading comprehension lessons, social studies, science.

This pupil-leader program helps many aggressive pupils learn to channel their leadership potential in a wholesome way. Some children who themselves have difficulty with their academic work display an amazing potential for leadership. They also have the ability to get other pupils to develop mastery in some basic skill subjects. In the process, their own skills improve.

At the start of the year, discuss the content of the subject areas with the whole class. Have the pupils sign up for those areas they are most interested in. Some will be remedial in nature while others will offer an enrichment opportunity. Some will be very popular and some pupils will have to settle for their second choice. Pupil-leaders can be chosen alphabetically until all the pupils get a chance at playing teacher.

On a typical day when this program is in operation, give the class some seat assignment so that you can spend five minutes with the four or five pupil-leaders. Your job is to make sure that each of them understands completely what it is you expect of them. Review the material they will be "teaching." Also, go over the general rules for the program. For example: pupil-leaders do NOT scold pupils or make belittling remarks. All pupils are to be treated fairly, etc.

This program, where tried, has proven quite successful. Pupil-leaders have gained new respect for their teachers and themselves.

Pupils who don't always relate well to their adult teacher respond better to a peer leader.

Some less ambitious programs for using pupils as teachers include: squad leaders, where a pupil is responsible for the behavior of a row or squad of eight pupils; homework checkers; lunch monitors; and gym captains. In each case, the pupil in charge feels a sense of responsibility that remains with him even when he is not in charge.

Can these ideas work in your classroom? The only way to find out is to try them. They've worked for other teachers and they should work for you if you adapt them to fit your class's needs and experiences. But, what if you don't have a class, in the sense that they are a group of disparate individuals, each pulling in a different direction? This is a growing problem. Teachers complain, "I can't make a class out of this year's bunch. It's always 'me, me' coming from thirty different directions. They don't even like one another!" You may need to get them to relax with one another and begin to feel comfortable with one another. This is a basic tool for solving classroom conflicts. In the parlance of your kids, they need to "hang loose."

loosening-up exercises that improve discipline

At the start of the school year don't assume that all of the pupils know one another. Form a circle and ask everyone his or her name. Add a simple but personal question, like: "What are you doing on Saturday?" or "What is your favorite snack?" Award prizes or points to the pupils who can go around the room and name every pupil correctly.

As a follow-up, or even as an alternate exercise, have pupils introduce their neighbors. Pupils are paired off and talk for five minutes. Each person talks about himself for about two minutes and then returns to the front of the room to introduce his partner to the entire class.

Try the interview game. One pupil plays an inquiring reporter who interviews the teacher and pupils selected at random. The reporter speaks in an official tone and pretends to take notes. After a few minutes, pupils form small groups in which everyone is interviewed. You might put a subject or provocative question on the board. The person being interviewed is made to feel important. His ideas are being sought and listened to. The other pupils focus their attention on him. It is his special time. This game is good for building confidence and a sense of community.

Adjective tags accomplish a similar goal. You first introduce the concept of adjectives and list a dozen or more on the board. Solicit adjectives from the class that describe a person. After a few minutes, erase the negative adjectives; you should have at least ten positive descriptive words on the board. Now ask the pupils, "Which of these adjectives describes something special about you?" Offer to add other adjectives that they might need help in spelling. Hand out 3″×5″ index cards with straight pins. Ask the pupils to select ONE adjective that they think describes themselves and wear it for the day. Just seeing the words, "kind" "friendly" or "loving" pinned to a pupil's shirt is an affirmative step.

With middle graders, a great icebreaker is the "Morse Code" exercise. It is nonverbal and so nonthreatening to the less articulate youngster. The class forms a circle, joins hands, and all close their eyes. You are part of the circle. The object of the exercise is for the person on your left to get the message that you send out starting with the pupil on your right. The message consists of hand squeezes and pauses very much like the dots and dashes of the Morse Code telegraph key. For example, you can give two squeezes, pause, and then one squeeze. After the message goes around the circle, the last person on your left squeezes your hand. This is a very unifying exercise since the whole circle is holding hands.

"Conflict Scenario" is a fine exercise to use in dealing with problem themes. Give the class a scenario and divide the pupils into small groups to find the solutions. Here are some examples:

A boy walks through the park with a basketball. An older boy takes his basketball away. What does he do?

A mother tells her daughter to come right home after school to babysit with her little brother. The girl forgets. When she gets home her mother is angry.

During a fire drill one boy tells another that his shoelace is untied. The rule is no talking during a fire drill. He is sent to the principal's office.

These warm-up lessons won't solve all your problems overnight. They will send you in the right direction. As you use them you will note changes in your pupils. There will be less tension in the air. The pupils will feel that they are part of a larger group.

a no-strings approach to puppetry

Some pupils find difficulty in relating to others directly. They seem to need a crutch of some sort. If only they could wear a mask in class they would participate more. We do not advocate the wearing of masks or even dark glasses in school. We do suggest that you use puppets as a medium to help pupils reveal their true selves and lower their protective shields.

"That doesn't scare me! I'm stronger and faster than you are. I'm the greatest boxer of all time. I can whip anyone in my class—in the whole school."

The puppet slid quickly along the table top. It was skillfully manipulated by the frail-looking boy whose teacher considered him shy, timid, and withdrawn. His classroom behavior indicated poor social skills. He hardly ever joined in group activities. Yet here he was, powerfully enacting a role, creating a new life, stronger than his own. Deeply engrossed in his task, he was participating in a group activity without fear or hesitation.

You can create the magic of puppets in your own classroom. They need not be professionally designed dolls but can represent the projection of life by the child into such unlikely forms as an old mitten, a paper bag, or a fragment of an old bed sheet.

Deep insight into classroom behavior is often brought to light through the behavior of the child during puppet play. Puzzling activities become more understandable to you, the teacher. You may have recognized an unusual response, but may not have been aware of the reasons for this behavior. Without an understanding of the motivating factors contributing to the pupil's behavior, it is hard to effect change.

The simplicity of materials is a big plus. A puppet figure may be the shadow of fingers and hands upon a wall or screen brought to life through the lively imagination of a pupil and the light of a filmless projector. A toy may assume character, and thus be transformed into an active puppet. A lump of clay modeled by the child's hand may become his teacher or parent. It doesn't matter if the puppet is of the string, shadow or hand variety. The use of impromptu performances frequently proves best for both the pupil and the teacher because of the opportunity for spontaneity in action.

Here is a list of puppets graded according to the level of sophistication. They can begin in Kindergarten.

Fist and finger shadows on the wall

Stick figures using ice cream sticks

Carrot, apple, and yam puppets

Rubber ball, cork, and sock puppets

Oaktag or paper one-string marionettes

Fist puppets of the mitten type

Balloon puppets

All-cloth string marionettes (3 strings)

Opaque shadow figures

Fist puppets with papier-maché heads

Marionettes with 5 or 7 strings

Translucent shadows made of acetate transparencies

When, through a puppet, a pupil has the opportunity to identify himself completely with another object for whose actions he will not be held responsible, you are given useful clues to his problems. A disturbed child can be referred to appropriate guidance personnel for help. Other members of the class may provide insight into their behavior patterns through puppetry. They may offer information which the teacher can use to help the child in the classroom. Spontaneous presentations offer the advantage of spur-of-the-moment responses and a comparatively free atmosphere. The pupil may reveal his feelings because he has not had time to organize evasive answers.

Puppetry dramatizations may be related to the class, school, or home situation. They can even relate to the curriculum. Here is a partial list of some successful situations dramatized with puppets.

New pupil in class

Dinner at our house

First day of the summer vacation

Christmas morning

My saddest day (happiest)
The school dance
When Daddy comes home
My best friend
Me, in five years.

The making of the puppets and care of puppets can be a learning experience for your pupils as well.

In this chapter we have tried to give you ideas employing games or activities that simulate real life. Some come from the human potential movement of the sixties. Others—dramatics, puppetry, skits— are techniques you've no doubt used before. We suggest here that you use them differently— with a focus on discipline. These simulations can help your pupils to see themselves in a positive way. They can help you to see your pupils as they really are—not as mere "pains in the neck." Use them to focus on conflict themes. Try them in small groups before you attempt to use them with the whole class. In any case, try them and adapt them.

12

overcoming vandalism and violence

The toll of vandalism and violence in American public schools adds up to more than $600 million annually, enough money to hire 50,000 teachers or pay the nation's entire bill for school textbooks!

A recent United States report indicated that there are over 70,000 serious physical assaults on teachers each year, and hundreds of thousands more against students. While certainly not every school in the country is faced with serious crime problems, it is clear that all teachers should be aware of the potential problems and take steps to prevent them.

There are steps that schools can take. Five years ago the Riverdale, California Elementary School was experiencing a break-in almost every weekend. A favorite target was the school's windows. Today, vandalism is almost nonexistent. A new approach was instituted: a blend of individual attention to pupils and the use of harsh punitive measures only as a last resort. When the principal must be stern he says, "I make it a point to seek out and speak kindly to the child later the same day so the child understands he is still liked as an individual, though his actions are disapproved of." The point is to give pupils a good feeling about themselves, thus giving them a good feeling about their school, so they protect rather than vandalize it.

how to teach the economics of vandalism

When students vent their anger against school, this is a reaction as old as the first school house. Yet the destructive student is still missing the mark. His actions won't change the school situation. And the really sad part is that the defacement won't even help his frustrations, except temporarily.

Damage calls for restitution; the vandal must make some amends. Insist that the vandal, if caught, work a prescribed number of hours to make up for the damage. If state laws permit, insist that the parents pay to repair the vandalism.

Better still, teach the economics of vandalism as a means of prevention. In a math lesson, when you introduce verbal problems, instead of writing out a problem about a farmer and his produce try something like this: "One broken window pane costs $4.80. Last weekend there were 18 broken window panes. How much money was wasted repairing the broken windows?"

After doing a few problems of this kind try a follow-up with: "Tickets for the circus cost $3.50. How many tickets could be purchased for the money spent on broken windows?" The children will get the point immediately.

With older pupils you can go into the area of deployment of labor. For example: "It takes Dom three hours every Monday morning to clean up the broken beer bottles in our school yard. What are some other things our custodian could be doing at that time that would help us more?"

These efforts at subtle, or not so subtle, brainwashing will have an effect on most of the pupils in your class. But what about the more serious problems of violence? There too, you, the teacher, can take preventive steps.

how to prevent problems before they start

Each part of the school day and each location within the school presents distinct problems where intruders are concerned. The three critical times are the morning when teachers and pupils enter school, lunch periods, and dismissal.

In the morning there are two distinct dangers that confront schools. The first is early morning crime in which teachers are victimized in nearly deserted school buildings. Don't be a "too early bird." Most teachers are highly conscientious; they have many things they like to do in their rooms before the pupils arrive. Most vicious attacks on teachers have occurred during the hour before school opens. We recommend that you do not arrive more than a half-hour before classes begin.

The second danger of the morning comes as pupils enter the building. If yours is an elementary school, there will be parents escorting some of the children. This makes it very easy for intruders to slip into the building. Stand outside your room so that you can screen any adult who comes toward your room. If you are seated at your desk or writing on the chalkboard, anyone can come into your room before you are aware of it. Keep your purse in a locked drawer or closet at all times. Be sure the lights are on in your room and that your desk is in a spot that can be easily seen from the door. Most doors to classrooms have windows. Don't obscure the vision of someone in the hall by covering up the entire window with some seasonal display. Be sure that your principal or other school personnel can look into your room even when the door is closed.

An additional problem at lunchtime is that there is the need in many schools for teachers to supervise yards and play areas. Teachers who have this duty should be given a thorough briefing on emergency procedures and a rapid means to communicate the need for assistance should a dangerous situation develop. It's a good idea to check doors to see that they have not been tampered with or left in an unlocked position.

One cardinal rule for teachers' safety, and it's especially important during lunch time, is: never be alone for any extended period of time anywhere in the building. You may prefer to spend your lunch period alone in your room. It's restful and quiet and all your materials are there. It can also be dangerous. Invite another teacher to eat with you. Be sure to lock your door and don't open it unless you are sure of who is on the other side. This is especially true for female teachers. While sex crimes are rare, when they do happen it is in rooms where the teacher is alone. You can prevent such an attack by having someone else with you.

Dismissal problems are very much like entry problems. Most teachers are required to escort pupils to an exit. They then return to their rooms, and some like to stay there to correct papers or prepare tomorrow's lessons. You are the best judge of how late you can safely remain in the building. You should certainly be guided by the practices of your neighboring teachers. Don't be the only one left in your part of the building.

By taking some of these preventive steps, you will avoid a dangerous and unpleasant situation. Make sure you have a classroom door that locks. Another type of classroom intruder problem concerns pupils from other classes or schools who are having a "good time" invading classrooms and harassing teachers. A twist of your key will keep them out.

tips for suppressing anger

Why are some kids so violent and angry? The answers are vague and varied. All *we* can do is try to reduce tensions and suppress rage.

Anger has many faces. Sometimes anger is mild. Sometimes it is expressed in furious rage. A minor incident can trigger something that has been building up for days. Does this sound familiar?

"Yesterday something happened for which I'm still ashamed. Jerry, the class bully, was poking Charles in his side with a ball-point pen. Charles told him to stop but Jerry kept it up. Finally Charles reached over and punched Jerry in the chest hard enough to cause him to shout out. I turned from writing something on the board and asked, 'Who yelled?' When I discovered it was Jerry who caused the disturbance, I felt a strong force of rage go through me. The next thing I heard was my voice shouting, 'I've had it with you. Go to the office and don't come back.'

The minute Jerry left the room I lost my feeling of anger and began to feel embarrassed. I found it hard to look at the class. By now they were dead quiet. I felt inside, 'I had no choice. He made me do it. He pushed me too far.' "

You may have felt this way often. If you would like to have peace in your classroom, try some of these ideas.

1. Accept personal responsibility for some of what goes on in your classroom. It helps to ask yourself how much you are contributing to the hostilities. Talk to a colleague about his or her

perception of how you talk to pupils. Based on this observation, develop a plan for changing or modifying your own actions. For example, drop the sarcasm or avoid put-downs.

2. Release the physical tensions caused by anger. Anger is a form of energy that must be discharged in a safe, positive way. If it is repressed it comes out in some other form. Once you realize that you are angry you can begin to discharge the physical tension in a constructive way. Take the class downstairs and out of the building for a walk. During the minutes between periods walk to the far end of the building on an errand. Get out of your room and away from the scene of the "crime."

3. Put it in writing. Take a few minutes to write the offender about how you feel—ANGRY. Let all of your feelings out. Don't keep any residue of anger inside. Let the person know in clear, simple language how furious you are. Avoid being logical; be emotional instead. Indulge yourself in adjectives. Tell the pupil just what you would like to do. Once you have it all down on paper, fold it carefully, insert it in an envelope, address it and then tear it up and throw it away. You will be amazed at how therapeutic this technique is. Once the anger is expressed, it's easy to approach the problem rationally and with less emotion.

ways to discuss violence in school

The best means of dealing with violence is to deal with it as it arises in everyday situations. Question why Jane and Katy are fighting. You will hear such answers as, "She deserved it"; "She was in my way"; 'I wanted my comb back."

Ask if there are any other means of dealing with the occurrences that provoked the violent acts. One pupil recently replied, "It's stupid to hurt people for no reason. If people have trouble, they should talk about it." No doubt, in such discussions you will hear children make similar comments. Write them down on a piece of oaktag and display them in a conspicuous spot in the room. Pupils like to see their remarks quoted and displayed. Other pupils respond better to the comments of fellow pupils than they do to the teacher's pronouncements. Refer to these words of wisdom when such incidents crop up.

Try role playing sessions if kids indicate they have problems. Talk about alternatives to kicking, punching, hitting. Discuss hurting someone physically or emotionally. What can happen? How does it feel?

Start a daily program that raises questions of ethics, behavior, and punishment. Even pupils on the first grade level can be encouraged to speak their minds about activities that affect them. Discuss violence in TV, books, and life. Such discussions can help kids understand themselves and others and eventually lead to mutually satisfying relationships.

some devices for reducing trouble in halls and stairwells

Often, you can reduce violence in your classroom but not when your pupils leave the room for other parts of the building.

Insist on certain standards of behavior when your class moves from one part of the building to another. Don't walk through the halls as if alone and expect your class to trail docilely behind you. Instead, have them walk short distances ahead of you, stopping at fixed points.

In secondary schools, many assaults occur in hallways as teachers attempt to stop students whom they do not know. In schools with large enrollments, pupils have a cloak of anonymity. It's important that pupils be challenged in halls. Do it with some tact. Don't make the challenge an altercation. One suggestion is that teachers greet pupils amiably—a simple "Hello" or "Hi" can work wonders in relieving tension if it is accompanied with a pleasant expression. Then ask for their identification. Instead of threatening a pupil with, "Where are you supposed to be now?" ask instead, "Where are you going?" There is a big difference between the two questions. You can make the gulf even larger by the tone of your voice.

This is not the time to remind pupils that they are hurting themselves by cutting classes and wandering the halls. This kind of sermonizing is likely to arouse hostility and quick denials—or retaliation. If the pupil does not have a pass or other legitimate reason for being in the hall, report him to some other authority. Do not let him get away with it. Telling him to move along solves nothing and may lead to increased hall wandering. Firm and fair enforcement of rules is the best bet.

Where do youngsters get some of their ideas about violence and school vandalism? Many experts blame the media—especially television.

how to deal with TV violence

All forms of media deal with violence: books, comics, radio, TV, and the daily newspaper. Because of its great appeal to children and the many hours they spend viewing it, TV has been held responsible for much of the violence that pupils encounter vicariously. Switch from channel to channel—victims are knifed, shot, strangled and raped. Yet television violence does not stop with fictional programs. You, yourself, saw, on live camera, the assassination of Senator Robert Kennedy, saw newscasts of other assassinations, and viewed terrible atrocities on the six o'clock news during the Vietnam war. Even if your pupils were too young to have seen these events when they occurred, TV offers many documentaries and replays.

Newspaper headlines and magazine covers highlight violence all the time. Radio gives us up-to-the-minute reports on muggings, assaults, and murders. Gory comic books are readily available to large numbers of children. Children are familiar with martial arts such as Kung Foo.

Our job is not to put blinders on our pupils but rather to define, recognize, and de-fuse some of the violence that assaults our children. In some areas youngsters see violence on the street where they live.

Coping with violence on TV can lead to coping with violence in life. Help your pupils find meaning in their lives by opening up discussions about violence. Because children's literature is considered a more serious and responsible art form, introduce your pupils to books like, *Durango Street* (Dell), *The Upstairs Room* (Crowell), *Viva Chicano* (Dutton) and *Cross-Fire* (Pantheon). In these books, violence is dealt with in a straightforward, realistic way. But it relates to the lives of the people. Violence is not used as a sensational or provocative device.

Follow up by being open and receptive to frank discussion. In upper grades, "rap" sessions serve well. Try to elicit from your pupils what violence is. You will be amazed at their responses. In most classes they run the gamut from child abuse to a teacher who always yells. One class was discussing a local street gang that extorted money, destroyed property and mugged senior citizens. When the teacher asked why the class thought the gang members engaged in such behavior a common response was: to be important. The teacher asked if this was the only way to feel important. After some thought the pupils agreed that you didn't have to hurt people to be important. Other good ways of feeling important were brought up.

ways to reduce racial and ethnic tensions

Sometimes tensions between groups can lead to violence which can cause widespread disruption. While there are many steps that can be taken to correct such disruptions, we want to discuss a human relations prevention program. This program may have to go beyond the confines of your classroom and involve the use of a team approach.

First gather some essential information:

What is the size of the potential rival groups?

Where does each group tend to congregate? (Turf pattern)

Who are the official or unofficial leaders?

Do any of the usual troublemakers belong?

Keep your eyes and ears open for remarks that some of your volatile pupils may be making. Pass this information along to a school administrator. The most likely place for a flare-up to take place is the lunchroom. Here, most of the pupils can be found at one time, there is pupil movement, and there is a less structured climate.

A good school program includes:

A student leadership committee representing various groups

Regular meetings of this committee with team members

Feedback to the groups by committee members

Establishment of a rumor clinic to prevent panic

Dissemination of accurate information to reduce rumors

There are also many informal ways to prevent tensions from building. These include multi-ethnic membership on teams, clubs, and monitorial squads, and pupil participation in decisions that affect them. We know of at least one school where a riot broke out over the kind of music being played during lunch. One ethnic group wanted only disco while another group would tolerate only rock music. The principal had left this decision up to the teacher in charge of the lunchroom and the pupils had no voice in the choices.

Seating in voluntary, nonstructured situations is sometimes a problem about which you can do little. In many schools where pupils can choose their own seats in the lunchroom, the seating takes on a racial or ethnic character. Some groups just prefer to sit with one another and there is little that can be done to change this. Insisting on seating by class or alphabetical order will produce more integrated seating—though artificial.

how to get parent support

Jesse Jackson, the black leader, has proved that effective results can evolve from cooperation between parents and schools, cooperation achieved through hard work and common goals from both parents and teachers. While today many parents are working outside the home, there are many supportive functions which parents can and are willing to perform—IF they are asked. Never assume that because a child is "bad" his or her parent must be disinterested.

One popular way to reduce racial or ethnic tensions AND bring parents into the school is to hold an International Luncheon or Dinner. Each child brings in a quantity of food that is a specialty of his parents' native country or ethnic group. This can be embellished with flags of the countries and a follow-up consisting of a cook book made by the class. Parents who are home should be invited to attend if it is held in the daytime. An evening dinner will bring out more of the working parents. By providing a baby-sitting service in a nearby classroom, virtually all the parents can attend at night.

Too many parents find school buildings and school teachers too intimidating and bewildering. It is well worth the effort to break down traditional barriers between parents and school. PTA meetings and parent conferences can be held in centrally located buildings, such as churches, where parents are comfortable and at ease. Most parents are concerned over their children's progress or lack of it in the public schools. Yet the resources they represent have hardly been identified or tapped in many areas of the country.

Just because a pupil in your class is a poor reader don't assume that his parents are illiterate. Even if yours is the slowest class in the school you may be able to attract one or two mothers to come in twice a week to help you prepare materials or work with a small group of slow readers.

If you do find that the parents who are available possess few or poor reading skills themselves you can still involve them in your class program. Call on parents to sew costumes for a play, teach the class a bilingual song, show the children how to handle tools, demonstrate how to prepare a regional food dish, talk about caring for plants, give a talk on pet care. You don't have to be a reading expert to bring expertise to the classroom. You can be sure that a youngster is more likely to feel proud of a school that has hosted his mother.

Senator Birch Bayh of Indiana recently addressed a group of teachers and said: "Most of the problems that are manifested in assaults on teachers, running bulldozers through new gymnasiums, stealing hubcaps, and puncturing tires in parking lots—most are manifestations of problems related to the backgrounds of children, of parent-child relationships at home. And the school, a depository for all of our children, is a vehicle in which this frustration, this lack of social acceptability and discipline, is played out."

He pointed out that schools should be used as community centers. "For many kids school represents the power structure. It is the only part of the establishment that they are familiar with. Often their frustrations are taken out against the establishment—and that is the school." He would like to see school facilities—swimming pools, playgrounds, music rooms, shops, home economics rooms, language rooms, or whatever—used to bring in parents as well as pupils for activities. Then the school would not be a "manifestation of frustration" but a place where parents and children could look for self-fulfillment.

You, as a classroom teacher, cannot make such changes in your school or community alone. But, together with others you *can* bring about changes; welcome, long overdue changes. Don't hesitate to get involved in the social and community life of your school community. Word will soon get around that you are a teacher who cares.

In conclusion, no one wants to see our schools become armed fortresses. And yet, a recent study released by the National Institute of Education pointed out that junior high schools can be more dangerous for pupils than the streets! Now, if this horror is to be reversed, if schools are to become relatively safe places again, much is required. To make these changes we must involve the pupils. To omit them would be disastrous. We must take steps to make these changes now. The alternative is not pleasant to contemplate.

This tremendous project will start tomorrow in your classroom. You can be the pebble that starts an avalanche. What you do does make a difference. If it is good it may spread. The world needs more teachers who try! Be alert, however, to "heavy" problems that do arise. Don't hesitate to call for help if a child pulls a knife or an intruder gets into your room. These things, unfortunately, do happen. We need you—don't become an injured hero or heroine!

13

discipline and the reluctant learner

If someone asked you, as you walked into school, what kind of day you were going to have, would you answer: "I don't know. I will have to wait and see how my third period class is going to act."? (An elementary school teacher might substitute "Nancy, Gerry, or Philip" for the third period class.) We hope you have never said this to anyone; not even to yourself.

Such an attitude causes us to give other people, our pupils, the power to make or break the day for us. What we are really saying is that we have no course of action, but that we wait until some reaction sets in. To go through a whole day simply reacting to what a nine- or sixteen-year-old is going to do is ridiculous. You can break this circuit by having plans for the reluctant learners as well as for the more avid learners in your class. Keep at your fingertips a "bag of tricks" that will provide easy, but not babyish, work for even the slowest pupil in your class. In this chapter we will show you how to handle these—the most challenging of pupils.

how to handle the underachiever

This is the pupil who, frequently, decides in advance that a situation is too difficult. He becomes petrified and freezes, or blocks, or shuts you out. If he is allowed to withdraw and retreat he will have fewer and fewer experiences and less growth will take place. The more situations that are avoided out of fear, the more fearful the pupil becomes.

There are a variety of ways you can help these kids feel that they can do the work. Here are a few:

1. Be sure the child knows exactly what he is supposed to do. Structure the learning situation so that he fully understands the process. An anxious pupil will worry about what might happen, what could go wrong, and how he might make mistakes. It is important not to assume that the pupil knows what to do just because you've been giving the same assignment all year.

2. Have the pupil compete with his own past performance rather than with any other child in the class. Eliminate peer pressure as far as you can. Ask him questions like, "How did you do as compared with last time?" or, "Is this what you expected to find on the test?"

3. Assure the pupil of success in learning. If a youngster is fearful of reading aloud in class, for example, have him tape his reading at home and play it back in class as a way of instilling confidence. Let him draw his book report instead of writing it.

4. At first, accept less. Reduce the criteria for success or correctness. Gradually raise your standards until he is able to meet the level of the rest of the class. You may have to hold the entire class to a reduced level.

Often, these children appear to be very arrogant. Don't let that arrogant attitude fool you. Underneath that haughty look and swagger is a very insecure, anxious child. These reluctant learners develop an attitude of "what if" this happens or that happens, when it comes to school work. This can be immobilizing; we need to help them see that, usually, the worst thing that happens is that we make a mistake and this only proves we are human beings. They will begin to see—perhaps for the first time—that their teacher is human, too.

tips on using visual approaches

Television has made it hard for some pupils to get excitement from the printed page when they can passively get similar enjoyment from the "boob tube." As teachers we have to try a variety of ways of getting our pupils "hooked on books." For a few, this is well nigh impossible. Martin was one such pupil.

His teacher explained that someday he will master the skills needed to complete the term paper project. But for now it was more important for him to learn an equally effective means of recording and reporting. She prepared and gave Martin an outline for a modified research report. His first assignment was to find out as much as he could about the local firehouse using a camera and a tape recorder. Taking pictures and talking into the battery-operated tape recorder would perform for him the same function that writing did for others. Martin used his outstanding verbal abilities to develop a tape-recorded narrative to accompany the slide presentation. His first attempts were acceptable but not outstanding, as you might expect. He was bright enough to improve quickly in the ability to take the pictures and tape an interesting report.

At the beginning he was given clear and simple objectives, along with a timetable for achieving these. If he met the timetable deadlines he was rewarded on a chart which listed each step. As he completed each step he could check it, but if he did it before or by the exact due date he earned a star instead of a check. Ten stars would mean a special reward. When he asked what his reward would be, the answer was another question, "What do you hope it might be?" The teacher made note of his answers; she now had time to decide which suggestion would have intrinsic value to Martin as a reinforcer and also a learning tool. She decided on Martin's most enthusiastic idea, "A role of film, to do what I want with." Also, she promised him he could then start work on a new slide-tape program on a topic of his choice. You never saw a more enthusiastic pupil! This time the teacher let Martin draw up his own timetable and plan for the content of the project.

The retarded reader and former reluctant learner blossomed with his new communications tools. At first Martin used all the pictures he took. Eventually he was able to select only the best from each set he had taken. Soon he learned how to go back and retake pictures with which he was disappointed. And about the middle of the year he started asking questions like: "Does this picture tell enough?" "Do I have enough pictures to tell the story?"

By the time the Easter vacation was over, Martin was actively and successfully producing high quality slide-tape shows. This visual approach gave him an ever-increasing amount of responsibility for setting his own goals and establishing timetables. Pretty good for a kid that other teachers had given up on!

how to use cross-age tutoring

At one point in his life, every child wants to play teacher. There are many occasions when every child could benefit from individual tutoring. Why not combine these two activities? Cross-age tutoring builds the egos of the tutors and gives the child receiving the help an extra bit of attention.

Try having upper graders listen to first graders read aloud, on a one-to-one basis. Start with one fifteen-minute period each week. Expand this as the children become comfortable with one another. The little ones will be thrilled with praise from anyone as big as a sixth grader. The older pupils, especially slow pupils, feel rewarded.

Sometimes the best person in the school to help a poor reader is another poor reader. Although poor pupils tend to have low frustration points, many of them show great patience in helping a less able pupil do school work. They find this less threatening than their regular school work. You will be amazed at how the older pupil will put word attack skills to work when working with his or her younger charge, thus reinforcing his or her own learning.

The "tutors" enjoy listening to first and second graders read aloud, on a one-on-one basis. Start your program on a schedule of one 20-minute period per week. As small successes are noted, expand to two or three periods per week. Be sure to keep the periods no longer than 20 minutes. The little ones will be thrilled with praise and recognition from the "big kids." The older pupils will feel rewarded by the experience. They will also parrot and echo the kinds of comments they have heard their own teachers use. You, the teacher, will be amused at hearing what comments and compliments the "tutors" use when working with the younger children. It may give you a sense of *déja vu*.

how to make the reluctant learner aware of school rules

You can minimize discipline problems if you develop an awareness on the part of slower and reluctant learners of just what the school rules are. Rules concerning pupil conduct should therefore be clearly stated in writing and distributed to everyone at the beginning of every school year.

Like everyone else, pupils are more likely to understand, respect and obey rules which they have had a part in formulating. Representatives of the student body, including some of the cutters, truants, and other reluctant learners, should work together with the staff to determine codes of behavior and establish an enforcement system.

These guidelines should be sufficiently specific to enable pupils, parents, and teachers to know what is expected in terms of conduct and discipline in the school. These should be reviewed periodically.

In junior and senior high schools, the standards of conduct which are established must not infringe upon the constitutional rights of the pupils. (Of course, they must not do this for elementary school pupils either; it's just that rules for young children are less likely to do so.) It is not necessary to prescribe disciplinary action for offenses committed within the school which are already adequately provided for by criminal law, unless the presence of the pupil in school would be a danger to the pupil himself, or to other members of the school community, or would disrupt the educative process. The school may not punish a pupil for offenses occurring off school grounds unless it can be established that such offenses are directly related to the orderly operation of the school.

Recently, the courts in New York State ruled in the *Matter of Wilson*, 11 Education Department #208:

> "Disciplinary action should not be predicated upon so nebulous a finding as 'lack of good citizenship,' a term which is undefined and which may be interpreted by reasonable men in completely different ways. It is, of course, a major responsibility of the school system to inculcate in students a basic respect for an adherence to the principles of good citizenship. This is an essential portion of the learning process. However, it is educationally unsound for a school system to brand an individual with the label of 'poor citizen.' The placing of such a label upon a student is not a proper function of the school system."

It is essential, we feel, that every pupil be aware of the school rules before we can accuse him of breaking them. Too often, teachers with middle class values assume that pupils from other backgrounds know instinctively what we find acceptable and what we find unacceptable. Pupils from other economic and social levels have a different tolerance for certain behaviors. Be sure to spell out just what is acceptable in your classroom and what is a "no-no." After you do that, go ahead and insist on compliance. You will find that it helps if you explain the "why" of your rules as well. Be sure to keep good records; you will need them if ever a court case emerges.

what to do when you must exclude the pupil

Don't you sometimes want to "get rid of a kid?" Wouldn't it be great if we could expel discipline problem-children without any fuss? In most states a pupil between 5 and 21 years of age who has not received a high school diploma is entitled to a free public education. If a board of education seeks to exclude a student from instruction, it may do so only in accordance with the statutes on the books. Yet, you may have one or more pupils who would benefit from a few days to cool off.

Preferably, minor disciplinary problems are handled within the school by teachers, with the principal handling the more serious disciplinary problems which could result in suspension. A teacher cannot suspend a pupil in most of the fifty states. The principal may suspend a pupil for a period not to exceed five school days where the board of education has adopted a bylaw which permits him/her to do so. Otherwise, only the board of education or superintendent has the power to suspend pupils.

Get smart and learn these surefire reasons accepted in most districts for pupil suspension. If one of your pupils fits into one of these categories, begin now to document specific infractions. Keep a log and jot down specific, concrete examples of what he/she does.

The following pupils may be suspended in most places:

- a pupil who is insubordinate or disorderly, or whose conduct otherwise endangers the safety, morals, health, or welfare of others

- a pupil whose physical or mental condition endangers the health, safety, or morals of himself or others
- a pupil who, as determined in accordance with the provisions of the law, is feebleminded to the extent that he cannot benefit from instruction.

No pupil may be suspended for a period in excess of five days unless he/she and the parent shall have had an opportunity for a hearing. The notice of the hearing should advise the pupil of the grounds for the charges in specific enough terms to enable him/her to anticipate reasonably the subject content of the proposed hearing.

Note the difference: your principal can suspend a pupil for up to five days on informal charges. If the suspension is to last longer, or if an expulsion is sought, then a formal hearing and much documentation is needed.

If the pupil is not absolved of the charged acts of misconduct, he/she may appeal the findings and determination of the superintendent to the board of education. Where the local board of education has, itself, made the determination, a pupil may further appeal either to the Commissioner of Education or to the courts.

In *Goss* v. *Lopez*, the United States Supreme Court stated that, in connection with short-term suspensions, a pupil should be given oral or written notice of the charges against him and an opportunity to explain the evidence and present his side of the story before a suspension is imposed.

So, don't take pupil suspensions or exclusions lightly. You should carefully evaluate your own situation. If there is a child who is preventing the other children from learning, reread the criteria we have cited. Continue to observe the child and write down the instances of his/her bizarre behavior. After you have some specific written documentation, go to the principal and state your case. Good luck!

ways to make your lessons more relevant

We continue to be amazed to find teachers who do all sorts of interesting things during their after-school hours yet remain dull and stilted when teaching their pupils. Most teachers don't think of sharing these fascinating interests with their pupils because "it's not in the course of study."

If gourmet cooking, World War II, or filmmaking is very important to you, why not use your interest in this area to vitalize whatever you're doing with your kids? There are so many varied ways to approach the same goal, and a little bit of creativity in getting there can go a long way toward making the classroom a more exciting and more down-to-earth place for you and the children you teach.

Many of the mini-courses or projects you pursue in the classroom may be suggested by the pupils themselves or by some unexpected incident that occurs. Someone brings in a coin from a foreign country or a snake, goes on a trip, wonders about an election, or where veal comes from—and you're off.

There will be times when that kind of spontaneous interest just won't be generated. That's when it's great to have some project you've thought through and developed to fall back on. And what could be better than a project that is your pet interest?

If we aren't excited about what goes on in the classroom, how can we expect the children to be? What are the essential ingredients of a good, relevant unit or project?

1. It has to be something that has a good chance of exciting the children's interest and that they can deal with on their own level.

2. It should provide many opportunities for activity and actual use of concrete materials: constructing models, collecting objects, making things, taking trips.

3. There should be some clear sense of what the goals of this project are and these should be stated in your plan.

4. The project should provide the maximum opportunity for extension in a variety of directions, depending on the children's interests. E.g., a unit on ecology could lead to air pollution and then to the automobile industry, then mass transportation, then to lifestyles, and so on.

5. This requires a great deal of preparation on the part of the teacher. Prepare equipment and books needed ahead of time. Have everything at your fingertips.

You won't be able to predict what will happen with your class. That is part of the excitement. You don't want a straightjacket approach that will prevent the following-up of the unexpected, but again, it is important to anticipate as much as possible the kinds of things that might occur so you won't be caught off guard. Such an approach will give you a greater lift than a shot of Vitamin B-12!

suggestions for making learning more individual

One of the guilt pangs that many experienced teachers feel concerns the matter of individualized instruction. Some of the questions frequently asked are: How do I get started? What kind of classroom space is needed? Does every kid have to do something different? Do I need to buy all new materials? Will I have to keep a lot of records? Do I have to spend all my time testing?

We'd like to show you one way to individualize—without pain. It is the "learning stations" approach. They allow pupils to work together at well-defined and self-directed lessons. Here are some easy steps to lead you on your way:

1. Plan your classroom environment. Set up listening areas, activity areas, and various corners (science, art, music).

2. Arrange the books and materials you already have in your classroom according to subject areas. Now, color code them. This will enable your pupils to return materials to the right place.

3. Prepare a simple profile on each child. List reading scores, observation notes, informal test marks. List the pupil's interests, weaknesses and strengths.

4. Get your pupils to help you set up rules of behavior for the learning stations. Ask them to plan procedures for sharing materials, following directions, etc.

5. Schedule learning station work. Decide where you want the children to work, and then list the children's names at the stations or on a central bulletin board.

6. Use contracts—formal or informal agreements between pupil and teacher—to decide which tasks at which stations will be done within a certain time limit. It's important to provide options so that the child has a part in the decision-making process.

7. You may want to use learning stations for only part of the day. There's always room for whole-class and group instruction in an individualized program.

8. Share the record keeping with the pupils. Many stations can be self-checking. Pupils can use peer checks, as well as checkoff

sheets, at the stations. If you use individual contracts, include space for the pupils to check off work done.

This above all—remember to go slowly. You are more likely to succeed if you take your time. Try one or two learning stations a week. Be sure to evaluate the stations with the pupils before going on to a new one.

Don't be afraid to ask for help. It's difficult to do everything by yourself. Get help from other teachers, older pupils, parents, and teacher aides. Of course, let your own pupils pitch in, too; it's the surest way to get their cooperation. "Interning for Learning" is another program that works well. Ask your colleagues about it.

By using these various strategies you will be able to get even the most reluctant learner to try a little harder. As with so many things in life, if only they would take the first step, the rest of the journey would be so much easier! Don't get discouraged. Just when you think nothing will work, some little thing will ignite that first spark. After that, things will go more easily. Good luck!

14

exercising control as a coverage teacher

Mrs. Harmon is an English teacher who has learned to control her five classes in an inner city junior high school. She is, by her own admission, not the best disciplinarian in the world. But, since September she has managed to exercise adequate control in her five classes—the pupils know her and have accepted her leadership in the classroom. Today, Mrs. Harmon found a "coverage slip" in her letter box. One of the math teachers has been excused to attend a conference and Mrs. Harmon has to cover one of the classes during her duty period. She panics because she never saw these pupils before and she doesn't think they will listen to her.

Does this sound familiar? This chapter will show you how to deal with this problem.

how to assume dominance within the first five minutes

It is traditional for a class to test a covering or substitute teacher. Individual pupils may try to gain status by upsetting class routines at your expense.

Your response to this kind of testing should be firm, tempered with good humor. Your object should be to return the class to an even level as quickly as possible. If seriously disruptive behavior on the part of one or two pupils continues, it would be wise to seek help from a teacher, a counselor or a supervisor who knows the pupil.

All kinds of things may cause disruptive behavior on the part of individual pupils. Some of them may relate to their interaction with you and the class; others may not. There are a few classic causes which can be responded to with some success by the sensitive teacher.

1. Boredom

If he doesn't understand what is happening in the classroom or if he has lost interest, the pupil may become bored and try to distract others. His behavior will be such as to call attention to his lack of participation.

2. Home Problems

The pupil may still be responding to some difficulty he has faced at home, either with his family or on the street. He may be worried, frightened, or just angry and upset.

3. Volatile Personality

A pupil's reaction sometimes seems to be disproportionate to what seems to be the cause. "You're picking on me."; "He called my mother . . . ": "He took my . . . "; "He started it."; these are familiar to all teachers. Generally they are just the sparks which serve to ignite a pent-up charge.

4. Pressure

Sometimes a pupil faces pressure which is not readily apparent. This may come from relationships within his peer group. Sometimes the pressure may be socio-political in origin.

5. Others

It would be impossible to categorize all of the potential causes of disruptive behavior. And when trouble breaks out, it is too late to diagnose. Experienced teachers often know when to ignore certain disruptive behavior, when to redirect a pupil's classroom activity, when to isolate, and when to seek help. A substitute teacher who meets a class for the first time would need an unusual amount of experience and sensitivity to be able to judge what is happening, and how to head off further difficulty.

"How can I prevent trouble before it starts?" is a question often heard. Certain combinations of planning, awareness, and sensitivity on the part of the covering or substitute teacher go a long way toward preventing disruptive behavior in some classes. The following suggestions have been found to be helpful.

1. Dispel Anonymity

Put your name on the board and leave it there. With seating charts, name plates or any other device that works for you, learn names quickly, and call pupils by name whenever possible.

2. Anticipate

Cluttered desks, scissors and rulers lying around, paper, paint, and chalk can all become attractive nuisances. If they can unobtrusively be put away until they are needed, potential trouble can often be avoided. A moment or two of thought before giving a flat "no" to a request can often make a great difference in the tone of a classroom.

3. Maintain Interest

Watch for signs of boredom. If only one or two pupils seem to have lost interest, they may become involved by taking notes on the board, or performing some other task. If many seem uninterested, the character of the lesson must be changed.

4. Don't Threaten

If action has to be taken, take it. Don't threaten, and don't promise to do what you cannot do. Sometimes a minor action taken early, judiciously, and swiftly can mean the difference between a controlled class and a mess.

5. Divide and Conquer

If you can see that a fight is brewing, or if one pupil is consistently troublesome, change some seats for the remainder of the activity. The troublesome child can be put to work at or near your desk. If for any reason a situation has gotten out of hand and you feel that you need help, send a pupil, with a note if possible, to a neighboring teacher or the principal.

6. Involve Others

You may find that a student teacher, an aide, or some other non-teacher has developed a relationship with some of the more troublesome pupils. Don't hesitate to give them a chance to take the troublemaker aside.

how to handle a class you never saw before

Don't be afraid to ask the pupils about the teacher's regular routine for checking homework and try to follow that routine. Both for continuity and for evaluation by the regular teacher, the covering teacher would be wise to give a similar homework assignment to be brought in for the regular teacher the next day. Most schools have a homework policy, and information on this policy can generally be obtained from a supervisor. A note should be left for the regular teacher indicating the homework assignment that has been given.

Teachers are very interested in learning what the class has covered in their absence. They are also interested in the performance of particular pupils who need further motivation to cooperate more fully with a substitute teacher. Either a special note, or a message on a form which the office provides, can be left in the teacher's mailbox. If special suggestions must be made for follow-up, tell the regular teacher. For example, "John did not do his board work on Thursday."

Here are some "do's" and "don't's" that will be helpful.

Do

Keep the class session from being monopolized by just a few pupils. Provide opportunities for all to participate.

Control the use of chalk and erasers. Make sure the pupils do not have access to them as weapons.

Make assignments commensurate with ability.

Be on time. By getting there before the class you will be in control. By coming late you will have to work twice as hard getting control back from the class.

Adjust your language and thought patterns to the level of the particular class.

Figure 14-1

Don't

Talk to the board. Your class is in the other direction.
Falsify your own personality by faking toughness or extreme friendliness. Just be yourself.
Be afraid to admit that you don't know the answer because this is not your regular subject or grade.
Show favoritism or use sarcasm.
Become so entranced with this new subject matter that you forget the class.
Allow yourself to be constantly sidetracked.

Figure 14-2

what to do if you expect to be absent

There is nothing worse than having a coverage or substitute teacher take over your class for a day or two and mess up everything you have tried to accomplish all term. You never know when you won't be in school the next day. So, plan ahead and prepare for substitutes by constructing a "survival kit" now. Then leave it out in plain sight on your desk each night. We think the following components are important to ensure that things go smoothly. Include other information that relates specifically to your classroom.

1. Seating charts and notes on individuals including nicknames, learning disabilities, health problems, potential troublemakers and usually dependable pupils.

2. Classroom procedures such as how you handle free study time or what happens during art, recess, physical education or reading periods. Where do your groups sit? On which days of the week do they go to the library, gym, science room, etc.?

3. Indicate where materials are stored, where keys to locked cupboards are kept and what things have to be requested. Also, don't be afraid to indicate what materials you don't want disturbed.

4. Extra work for fast finishers. Draw up a list of projects or refer to folders of duplicated assignments that can be passed out.

Remember that uncertain substitutes invite trouble and that without your help substitutes won't be able to perform their duties capably or professionally. Although this kind of planning may take some time and organization, your efforts will be well rewarded. The substitute will work harder for you, your students will enjoy a better learning atmosphere and you can pick up where you left off with a minimum of disruption.

suggested surefire lessons for any class

Some teachers have less difficulty than others in covering a class. Many experienced teachers have acquired a kind of repertoire of surefire lessons that they can adapt for almost any situation.

These are certain lessons which have proved to be especially interesting to pupils. They may come from any subject area, but particularly from one in which the teacher has a special competence or interest. The following suggested lessons may be adapted to any school level.

1. Penny Archaeology: Pupils are asked to imagine that they are archaeologists a thousand years from now. They found a penny in the ruins of an American city. What could they learn from this penny? (Language, religion, architecture, calendar, clothing, coinage, metallurgy, etc.)

2. Personalized Time Line: Pupils enjoy making time lines of family history or events in their own lives. Have them draw a horizontal line and draw points on it that represent milestones in their lives.

3. Take One or Make One: After asking pupils whether they would rather take a test or make one up, (and receiving the expected answer) set some ground rules for constructing a test, and have the class go to it. Ground rules should include the scope of the subject area to be covered, the length of the test, and a sheet of correct answers so that at a future time the test may be given and marked. Textbooks should be used in test construction. This provides an excellent review lesson.

4. Book of Lists: Ask pupils to take a page in their notebook and make a list of animals. The longest list wins a prize. Next, ask them to list all the words they can think of that describe the weather. How many 20th century inventions can they list? For slower classes, ask pupils to list everyday items such as boys' names, foods, TV programs, etc.

5. Creative Problems: What would happen if people never died? If cars never wore out? If it always rained on Saturday?

6. The Future: Pupils are asked to describe food, clothing, shelter, travel, and entertainment as projected for the year 2222 A.D.

7. A Pupil Directory: Every pupil in the class can help to make an alphabetical list of class members. Decisions can then be made regarding what to add (addresses, phone numbers, siblings, languages spoken, favorite stars, etc.).

13 ways to prevent chaos while you cover a class

Occasionally, no matter how hard you try, trouble breaks out. Here are suggestions for handling it effectively.

1. Experiment with various teaching personalities until you find the right one for you. Alter your personality to fit the class. Some classes need more rigidity and structure.

2. Let the pupils know exactly what you expect from them and demand no less.

3. Gain control. When a situation lacks control and students become rebellious and aggressive, don't be afraid to sacrifice the lesson. Continue the lesson only after order has been restored. Do this by stopping the lesson and waiting for silence. Remove pupils who prevent order.

4. Many pupils have short attention spans. Redirect activities whenever children show signs of uncontrollable restlessness. If a lesson doesn't work, save it instead of trying to complete it for the sake of your lesson plan.

5. Pupils need a sense of order in their lives, although they sometimes react in the opposite way. Clearly define your guidelines.

6. Learn to ignore certain things. It's an effective way to allow a pupil to come to terms with his or her own behavior. Reacting to every minor incident and attention-getting device only serves to stop the learning process and snowball the incident.

7. Misconduct should be stopped in its early stages through the use of body language. Set up certain signals—nods, pointing, disapproving looks—to show that whatever is occurring should be controlled.

8. Watch your temper, but let children know that when you're angered, it's a prelude to another form of punishment if they don't heed your first warning.

9. Learn voice control and use it as a disciplinary tool rather than as an emotional outlet.

10. Carry through all threats, but never make unreasonable or unwarranted ones.

11. Do not show favoritism. Perhaps only one or two pupils in the whole class are your link to sanity; don't use them as examples, but, rather, have them serve as tools in working with the others in tutorial capacities.

12. Use praise lavishly but sincerely. Pupils recognize false praise and lose respect for its giver.

13. Very often a little humor will de-fuse even the worst discipline problem. Don't be afraid to kid the pupil along.

This baker's dozen will get you through even the roughest class in your school. Speaking of rough classes, and rough schools, you must be aware of sensible security precautions. The statistics get worse all the time concerning teachers getting hurt IN school. Don't become a statistic.

security measures you must take

As a classroom teacher you cannot assume responsibility for the security of your school building. You can, of course, get some of your colleagues to go with you when you speak to your principal about the need for definite procedures and precautions. These include the obvious, like a parent-volunteer at the door on the days when the security guard is absent. Or, the need for a code message on the loudspeaker when an intruder has been spotted in the school. The code message may take the form of "Miss Hendricks, please report to the office" when no Miss Hendricks is on the staff. Upon hearing such a code message each teacher would lock her classroom door and allow no pupil to leave the room. A member of the administrative staff would check all the toilets to locate pupils already out of the room.

Get in the habit of keeping an "Out of Room Book." This can be a simple notebook attached to your room door with a piece of string. Whenever a pupil leaves the room he or she signs out with the date and time. In this way you can check to see who is out of the room at any time. Also, if an incident takes place and one of your pupils was out of the room at the time you will have an idea as to the possible culprit.

Be discriminating. Assume all responsibility for persons you permit to enter your room. Ask a parent for her name and the name of her child before you allow her to come into your room. If she is a legitimate visitor, she won't mind giving you her name and will appreciate your vigilance. If he or she has no business in your room, don't hesitate to send the person to the office. Never let a visitor remove a child from your room without written authorization. This is one area where you should pass the buck. There are many families in which one parent has custody over a child and the other parent is denied any visiting rights, or has limited rights. Don't get into a situation where you send a child home with his father when the court has awarded custody exclusively to the mother. Irate parents can present a security problem for you and your class under these circumstances.

As a general rule, don't allow children to leave the room unless it is a dire emergency. Hall traffic breeds trouble. If they must leave, send them in pairs. Use a wood or cardboard room pass so that you can see at a glance if one pair is already out of the room. You may want to set up further limitations, such as, "no one leaves the room immediately before or after lunch."

By limiting the occasions when pupils leave your room, you achieve a secondary gain—you can keep your classroom door locked. Teaching behind locked doors will give you a sense of security. If your room door has a glass window, keep it free from decorations. Staff members passing through the hall should be able to see in easily and thus report any untoward incidents.

If your pupils are old enough, simulate incidents and have pupils discuss possible lines of defense. Point out how help can be summoned without danger to pupil or teacher. This must be done in such a way that pupils do not have night terrors.

Review your procedures for securing your coat and valuables. Be sure you do not tempt pupils by keeping a handbag, watch, coat, or other valuables out in the open or unattended. Insist that the administration furnish you with a desk or closet that locks. If necessary ask the custodian to put a hasp on a closet door and you buy your own padlock.

Fortunately, these are the exception rather than the rule. Let's end our chapter on a more positive note.

hints for making coverages less harrowing

Try a team teaching approach. This can be especially helpful in cases of special coverages (gym, foreign language, shop, etc.). By teaming two or more classes, the experienced teachers and the covering teacher can approach teaching in a less orthodox fashion than usual. One teacher can lead while the others assist, thereby combining both large and small group instruction in one lesson. Sometimes a student teacher majoring in the subject can provide assistance as a resource person, so long as there is a licensed teacher in the room.

Where the teachers in a grade or in a subject area function as a team, the grade leader, in cooperation with his colleagues, might work up alternative plans for a school day on which one or more of the teachers is absent and only one covering teacher is available. Here you can look forward to the use of the auditorium for the showing of films or filmstrips, science demonstrations, music lessons, interclass activities and programs which have proven successful in school assemblies, such as a quiz show.

The life of a covering teacher can be made more pleasant if all the teachers in the school observe these four rules:

1. Anticipate possible absence at any time: make available plans, keys, seating charts, materials, class lists, program cards, etc.

2. Establish class activities and routines enabling pupils to work more easily with another teacher: advance assignments, group and individual projects, a class secretary, help of student teachers, cooperative attitude on the part of pupils, monitor lists, class sets of labeled duplicated materials.

3. Support the covering teacher returning to class: follow up on homework assigned, noncooperating pupils, work covered during absence, etc.

4. Be willing to help covering teachers of other classes in your department or in nearby classes; answering questions, making informal suggestions, providing material, getting pupil cooperation, aiding in emergencies.

If all the teachers would follow these four precepts, every covering teacher would have a less harrowing experience. No matter how clear forms and materials may be, they are of limited value without the all-important dimension of personal help, encouragement and support.

Above all else, maintain a positive mental attitude toward this temporary assignment. This will rub off on the pupils in the classroom. And remember this—if this is a difficult class, think how happy you will be to return to your regular assignment. If it is a good class, make the best of this opportunity to teach rather than discipline. In any case, a month from now the experience will be ancient history. The regular teacher is stuck with them for the rest of the term.

15

solving
attendance problems
related to discipline

Two teachers were overheard in the lounge just before the start of school. One was heard saying: "I didn't see Gerald on the class line. I do hope this means that he will be absent today. I can use a break."

This kind of thinking is not fair to Gerald and, looking at it from the teacher's viewpoint, it is not in her best interest to promote non-attendance on the pupil's part. When there is a loss of continuity, the discipline problem gets worse and not better. He makes up for lost time on the days that he does come to school. Experienced teachers have learned to solve attendance problems related to discipline—and this has made their job easier.

checklist of proven classroom techniques

The school person most likely to have the greatest impact on a pupil is the classroom teacher. This teacher more than anyone else may be able to prevent unnecessary absenteeism and help pupils return to school. It is important that the classroom teacher do at least the following:

1. Regularly confirm addresses, apartment numbers, telephone numbers, and parent contact information. Some teachers, in calling the roll, ask pupils to respond with their address on one day and their

phone number on another day. By keeping this information up-to-date the teacher can help in the follow-up when the pupil is absent.

2. Require a note signed by a parent from all returning absentees. Keep these in a manila envelope until the end of the year. If attendance does become a problem you will have documentation for the times the pupil was absent from your class. Occasionally check the parent's signature on these notes and on the report card. You may find that some notes show a variation in signature and this will require some explanation on the part of the pupil.

3. Keep parents informed of their children's attendance. At parent conferences, refer to your roll book as well as your marking book. Parents may not be aware of all of their child's nonattendance. Ask the school office for a supply of post cards. Drop one in the mail when a pupil is out for an isolated day here and there. If the post card gets no reply, ask the school secretary to call the home or the parent at his or her place of business.

4. Use the supportive pupil personnel services within the school. By all means tell the guidance counselor if you suspect truancy. He may be seeing the parent about another child in the family and thus will have direct contact. Tell the attendance coordinator who can arrange for a home visit in case of sustained absence.

5. Consult with the attendance coordinator about absentees. Together you may come up with a pattern. Is the pupil absent mostly on days when the class goes to gym? Are Mondays and Fridays the days when the child is usually out? Do visits with a divorced parent trigger days out of school? Does the child have adequate winter clothing or shoes?

6. Talk to the school nurse about children who are out for long periods of time. Is there some chronic illness or condition? Does the child have all the shots that are required?

7. Develop a supportive atmosphere for returning pupils. Make the child feel comfortable when he returns to your class. Assign a pupil to go over some of the missed assignments with him. Hold a brief conference at your desk and inquire as to the child's perception of why he was absent. Sometimes an inconsiderate parent keeps an older child at home to watch a preschool child. See how the pupil feels about being kept home. Some overprotective parents keep a child home for long periods when a simple cold has already been treated. Make the pupil feel that you are glad he is back and that you are

concerned about his welfare even when he is away. This will make even the nastiest pupil feel that he is considered a human being by his teacher. This consideration and trust is sure to be rewarded. Don't ever let the child feel that life was so much easier for you during his absence, even if this was so. This is a self-fullfilling prophecy—the youngster will live up to the negative image you have of him. Don't fall into the trap of yielding to this temptation.

Even the most concerned teacher cannot work in a vacuum. Pupil attendance must become a team effort if any improvement is to be seen. For that reason, many schools have set up a School Attendance Committee.

setting up a school attendance committee that works

The Madison School has gone from one of the lowest percentages of pupil attendance in the district to one of the top three. When we asked some of the teachers how, they cited the SAC (School Attendance Committee) which meets every other month. In addition to the principal and a school aide there are two teachers and the president of the PTA. Here is a copy of their attendance plan which came out of their second meeting.

Attendance Plan

1. Daily listing of all absentees by the school aides.
2. Follow-up by phone if the reason for absence is not known.
3. Immediate home contact of known malingerers.
4. Principal checks each daily list. Parent conferences are arranged when a name appears too often.
5. Special programs are planned for pupils with very poor attendance. Reading volunteers work with these pupils as well as the Homework Helpers.
6. Contact is made with District Office personnel when indicated: attendance coordinator, guidance counselor.
7. The promotion sheets in June reflect knowledge gained about pupils during the past year. In this way next year's teacher is alerted at once.
8. An incentive program was set up to reinforce good attendance.

9. Monthly ribbon to the best attending class in each grade.

10. At assemblies, commendation cards are given out to pupils and classes with perfect attendance.

11. Posting of monthly class attendance averages.

12. Pizza party at the end of the year for the class with the best attendance, paid for by the PTA.

13. Improving school spirit through bulletin boards, teams, PTA newsletter, and club program.

14. Positive mental hygiene approach shown by all personnel in the school. "School is relaxed and a good place to be," said one of the counselees.

15. Attendance coordinator deals with all problems of attendance including busses, lateness, parent cooperation; custodial engineer understands the importance of heat, light, and cleanliness in making the school attractive.

By working together, this group of adults concerned with pupil attendance can and does make a difference. You can be instrumental in your school by bringing about a positive change when you suggest a multi-pronged approach to attendance. As one of the fifth graders said to his guidance counselor, "School is relaxed and a good place to be." The children who roam the streets or who hide at home are looking for a good place to be. You can provide that environment right in your classroom.

how caring teachers established a community relations program for effective school attendance

You can go beyond the walls of your school building as did the teachers from a Pennsylvania school we visited. These teachers felt that a closer tie between the school and parents should be developed. Parents' cooperation was requested through the newsletter and at meetings. They were urged to cooperate in such matters as not keeping children home unnecessarily, sending a notice to the school when the child is absent, returning absentee postcards promptly or telephoning the necessary information, etc. They prepared letters in Italian and Greek when necessary to insure total parent awareness.

Much absence is caused by parents and much more is inaccurately explained by parents. While, in most cases, the parent's statement is a reflection of fact, it may on many occasions also reflect personal problems, anxieties, indifference to education, lack of understanding of the school's purpose and the feeling that any statement will be accepted.

They worked closely with parent organizations and with parents who are not members of such a group. Parents and pupils were told the school regulations regarding the attendance of all pupils on the first day of admission.

Through talks at parent organization meetings and through the parent organization newspaper, parents were kept aware of regular attendance. The attendance teacher was invited to speak at parent meetings. Open School Week offered an opportunity to emphasize the need for regular attendance.

Letters and telephone calls to parents about excessive absence were found to be useful. Parents were invited to the school for an interview in cases of excessive absence where no improvement was shown.

In cases of prolonged absence, they kept in touch with the home so that the parent was aware that the teacher was interested in the child's welfare and in his early return to school. Other pupils in the class were encouraged to send notes and get well cards.

In June, a meeting of prospective Kindergarten and first grade children was held for orientation purposes. The importance of regular attendance was stressed at this time.

A welfare committee was set up to help needy families. This committee provided clothing, shoes, raincoats to children who lacked them and were therefore unable to attend school. Parents whose children attend clinics were urged to try to bring the children to school for part of the day, if possible. Parents whose children visit doctors for injections, orthodontia, etc. were requested to avoid, insofar as possible, appointments during school hours.

Such devices as parent education programs through the Parent's Association helped to inform parents of the financial loss entailed for the school, of the loss in learning time for the children, and of the need to develop wholesome attitudes toward school on the part of the children.

The teachers were rewarded with more consistent pupil attendance and improved behavior from pupils who rightly sensed, "my teacher cares."

It is when kids know that you care about them that self-discipline has a fertile ground in which to flourish. By all means, give these suggestions a try. Suggest to your principal that your school make improved attendance a priority this year.

how one school improved its attendance dramatically

P.S. 20 was built about seventy years ago and the school and the neighborhood have both seen better days. Yet, there are many young blue-collar families living in the community, and they want a quality education for their children. Most of the teachers have been at the school a long time and they were discouraged by the poor attendance of pupils in recent months. They embarked on a ten-step program

---

Date:

Dear Parents:

　　Once again I must ask your cooperation in the matter of pupil attendance. Our teachers are most anxious to have all the children benefit from the lessons they have prepared. It is difficult to have pupils make up work when they are absent frequently.

　　We urge all parents to keep pupils at home only when it is necessary for reasons of health. While we don't want pupils to attend school when they are ill we do want them to come to school on all other school days.

　　So far this year, your child ＿＿＿＿＿＿＿ has been absent on these dates:

　　Please check to see that you were aware of these dates. If you have any question, don't hesitate to call the attendance teacher at 761-1234. Since this letter is going out to all parents whose children were absent 15 or more days don't be offended by our request that you check the dates of nonattendance. There are some children who absent themselves without their parents' knowledge.

　　　　　　　　　　Sincerely,

　　　　　　　　　　Edna Verona
　　　　　　　　　　Principal

Figure 15-1

which we have excerpted for you complete with form letters. Here it is.

1. Letters we sent to all parents discussing the importance of regular attendance. (See Figure 15-1.)

2. If a child returned to school without an absence note, a form letter (see Figure 15-2) was sent home to the parent requesting the reason for the absence.

3. Special interviews with parents whose children had poor attendance, with the view towards determining the root cause, were held.

4. Teachers engaged in an art program related to the importance of attendance. Posters were designed fostering good attendance.

Date _____

Dear   :
      Your child _____ of Class _____ was absent from school on _____. It is the policy of the Board of Education to have every absence accounted for by receiving a note of excuse from the parent or guardian.
      Please indicate below the reason for this absence and return it promptly to the classroom teacher.
      Prompt and regular attendance is necessary for successful school work.
      Thank you for your cooperation.

                              Sincerely,

                              Edna Verona
                              Principal

— — — — — Please tear off and return to school — — — — —

Dear Miss Verona:
      My child was absent because:

Child's name: Class: Parent's Signature:

Figure 15-2

5. Teachers were told not to announce to their pupils that they would be absent the next day. Many pupils would take the teacher's announcement as an invitation to stay home.

6. Each day a child from a class with 100 percent attendance would come to the office to personally announce the good news over the loudspeaker.

7. An attendance banner was given each month to the class with the best attendance.

8. Children with perfect attendance were mentioned in the monthly PTA publication.

9. Award assemblies were held every month for all classes where children had earned attendance buttons.

10. A school aide was trained to make phone calls to parents of absent children daily. She also sent home post cards if no one answered the phone.

why you can and do make a difference

In the book *Fifteen Thousand Hours* (Michael Rutter et. al., Harvard University Press, 1979), four British educators argue that teachers can and do make a difference.

The researchers compared two public elementary schools located in similar low-income sections of London—schools A and B. At the beginning of the study, one-third of the incoming 10-year olds at both schools demonstrated problems such as truancy and vandalism. Four years later, however, the study concluded that fewer than 10 percent of the students at school A demonstrated attendance problems while 48 percent of the students at school B demonstrated such problems.

What makes some schools more effective than others? The study spells out few specific details, but it does conclude that the *general atmosphere* of the place has more effect on students than the age of the physical plant or how strict the discipline is.

Elements contributing to a productive atmosphere, the study said, include: emphasis on studies, the active and sincere involvement of teachers in lessons, the availability of rewards and praise for students, and emphasis on student responsibility—allowing them to see the consequences of their own actions. The study also concluded that results are generally better in schools where teachers play an active role in forming discipline policies and in development of curriculum.

These experts also found that the younger the students are when schools approach the problems of discipline and student attendance, the better the solutions will be. Two studies conducted recently with the support from the American Political Science Association reinforce that assumption. In these studies, researchers found that concerted efforts in Kindergarten through grade 8 are more effective than high school programs in developing good attendance and good discipline. The early years are when the students actually form values.

And so we see that the kind of atmosphere you provide for your pupils is a major factor in their attendance and their discipline.

We have all heard a great deal about the word "tone." You set the tone in your classroom. Tone is the general quality or atmosphere of a classroom or school. When we say, " . . . tone down," we are referring to making something less vivid, harsh, violent, etc.—more moderate. This is precisely what you want to do in your classroom— moderate the harsh or violent. By improving the tone of the room you are improving the lives of all of your pupils and yourself. Remember this tomorrow morning as your pupils enter the room. What kind of tone are you trying to establish? Are you setting the tone for the class or are they deciding what it will be? You can and do make a difference. Don't abdicate your role.

what do the kids say?

In gathering information for this book we frequently wondered just what the kids thought about all this.

Following a year of study, an 18-member Student Affairs Task Force submitted a lengthy report on discipline to the New York State Education Commissioner. In addition to earmarking successful programs, the report made overall recommendations on attendance. Here is the essence of their report:

1. Reward pupils who attend school and their classes. An example of such an award is giving free tickets to school events. Special rewards or awards may be given to students with outstanding attendance records on a weekly, monthly, or yearly basis.

2. Deny class-cutters certain privileges. For example, they may be denied the privilege of attending or participating in after-school activities for a specified period of time.

3. Inform parents of students who are truant or cut classes, immediately. It is important to involve parents in the school's efforts to eliminate that behavior.

4. Encourage students to assume responsibility for their behavior and to fully utilize their educational experience. Informal or formal discussions focusing on the necessity for self-discipline and for assuming responsibility for consequences resulting from their actions are strongly encouraged.

5. Offer a wide variety of elective courses which the students view as relevant to their lives and which are designed to satisfy their varying interests, needs and desires.

6. Utilize every opportunity and available resource for the purpose of expanding the classroom experience. Experimental learning is highly recommended.

7. Establish guidelines which are sufficiently specific, enabling students, teachers, administrators, and parents to know precisely what is expected in terms of conduct and discipline within the school.

8. Compile, in writing, all rules concerning student conduct and disciplinary practices utilized by the school. The printed material should be sent to all parents and distributed to all students at the beginning of each school year or at such time as they initially enter the school.

9. Avoid disciplinary action predicated upon so nebulous a finding as "lack of good citizenship," a term which is undefined and which may be interpreted by reasonable individuals in completely different ways.

10. Abolish out-of-school suspension, except in cases of violent crimes, and replace it with in-school suspension programs whenever suspension is appropriate.

11. Incorporate some form of rehabilitation into every type of discipline practice or strategy. A rehabilitative procedure for students in in-school suspension may be the formulation of a behavioral contract written by the student and agreed upon by the other party or parties involved in the incident which led to the student being placed in in-school suspension.

12. Teachers should be responsible for initial communication to parents when problems arise in the classroom.

As you read these pupil-inspired recommendations, you see that the apple doesn't fall far from the tree. These are pretty much the same things we have been hearing from teachers and parents.

a case study

Wilson Junior High School is in a changing neighborhood. The middle class families have moved further west. The once stable neighborhood is now peopled by families on public assistance. Many fathers are out of work and can be found in the parks during the day. There are also many school children roaming the playgrounds during school hours. In spite of this general malaise there are many intact families and fatherless families "making it" by dint of hard work and good fortune.

Attendance is averaging only 78 percent with even fewer pupils present on Mondays and Fridays. There have been three principals during the past four years. The teachers are assuming more of a leadership role and have introduced many successful programs geared to improving pupil attendance. After six months the percentage of pupils present has jumped 10 points. Some of their efforts include the following:

Pupils with poor attendance are placed in a special counseling class where the importance of good attendance is stressed. Successful citizens from the community are brought in to speak with pupils about the reasons for having a good education.

Pupils are offered remediation in their school work by the counselors during these class sessions.

A reward system has been set up for the homeroom with the highest average daily attendance during each attendance period. The homeroom with the highest average daily attendance receives a special field trip.

Special activities have been planned for Mondays and Fridays since these days were identified by the school as having the highest rate of absenteeism.

Motivational posters such as a graph of attendance and certificates of recognition for attendance are displayed throughout the school.

Homeroom teachers are encouraged to telephone the parents of absentees and record the reason for absence on attendance cards, which are reviewed by the attendance coordinator.

The school has established a teacher advisory group whose purpose it is to develop better communication among administrators, teachers and pupils on attendance goals and problems.

The school sends out letters twice a year reminding parents of the importance of their children's good attendance in school. New students are immediately issued copies of the school schedule along with a note to their parents informing them what is expected of their children in relation to school attendance.

We have tried to show you in this chapter that there is no single way to improve attendance. There is no single way to improve discipline either. If there were, there would be just a single book on the subject and every teacher would commit it to memory.

*   *   *   *   *

On this page, we would like to leave you with a few simple rules that should get you started on the path to a sane and safe classroom.

Emphasize doing – not doing perfectly.

Use your energy for action – not for worrying.

Learn from others – right in your building.

Be persistent – don't give up!!!

index